COINS YOU CAN COLLECT

COINS
YOU CAN
COLLECT

NEW AND REVISED EDITION

by Burton Hobson

Illustrated with photographs

HAWTHORN BOOKS, INC. • PUBLISHERS • NEW YORK

ACKNOWLEDGMENT

The author wishes to thank *Coin World/World Coins*, P.O. Box 150, Sidney, Ohio, for information on foreign mints that provide numismatic services. *Coin World/World Coins* has available a nominally priced list of coins available direct from various foreign mints, their prices, and order information.

NEW AND REVISED EDITION

1 2 3 4 5 6 7 8 9 10

To
Alice, Andy and Mark—three certain
future coin collectors

CONTENTS

Introduction	9
How to Get Coins	13
How to Store and Display Coins	15
Handling Coins	17
Coin Values	18
Coin Publications	19
United States of America	23
Canada	27
Mexico	29
Bahamas	31
Bermuda	33
Jamaica	34
Netherlands Antilles	35
Haiti	37
Dominican Republic	38
Nicaragua	40
Panama	42
Guatemala	44
El Salvador	46
Costa Rica	47
Honduras	48
British Honduras	49
Brazil	50
Argentina	51
Uruguay	53
Colombia	54
Venezuela	55
Ecuador	56
Chile	57
Paraguay	58
Peru	59
Bolivia	60
Great Britain	61
Ireland	64

Channel Islands	66
Guernsey	66
Jersey	66
France	69
Monaco	71
Belgium	73
Luxembourg	75
Netherlands	77
Denmark	79
Sweden	81
Norway	83
Finland	85
Germany	87
Austria	89
Switzerland	91
Italy	93
Vatican City	95
Spain	97
Portugal	99
U.S.S.R.	101
Greece	102
Israel	104
New Nations of Africa	106
Ghana	106
Mali	106
South Africa	109
Japan	111
Nationalist China	113
Hong Kong	115
Australia	116
New Zealand	118
South Pacific Islands	120
Fiji	120
French Polynesia	120
Glossary	122
Index	126

INTRODUCTION

If you have heard that all interesting coins are expensive and hard to get, don't believe it because it just isn't so. Anyone can build up a worthwhile collection, have fun doing it, and learn many interesting things in the process.

Some coins, of course, are rare and costly: gold coins, for example, always bring comparatively high prices because the metal itself is of value. But value is not determined by price alone. Every coin in your collection, no matter how small its cost, can become valuable to you. Not only does each represent the story of how you came to acquire it, but the denomination itself represents the promise of a government to pay a specified amount, and a portrait or a coat of arms on the face of a coin can tell you something about the land it comes from.

The words that appear on coins are interesting too—many have legends in Latin, Spanish, French, German or Italian. By learning the meaning of these words, you can become somewhat of a linguist. The more you learn about the coins in your collection, the more precious they will become to you and to everyone with whom you share your knowledge.

The purpose of this book is to tell you about and show you the coins you *can* collect, easily and inexpensively. These are coins that are now in circulation in many different nations and colonies of the world. The coins were chosen either because they come from countries that people frequently travel to or because they are especially interesting or easy to obtain. You may well be able to get coins of other countries, too, or older issues from

9

these same countries. As time passes, new coins will come along to replace some of the issues described here. This book shows you the *kind* of information you can discover from coins and about coins.

Even if you don't actually collect coins but do like to travel or study geography, this book has something to offer you. Coins shown are those used today in other countries, the very coins that pass from hand to hand in daily commerce. If you are a traveler, you can familiarize yourself in advance with the coins you will encounter; and if you are a student, reading about these coins will give you an extra glimpse into life in other lands.

COINS YOU CAN COLLECT

these same countries. As time passes, new coins will come along to replace some of the issues described here. This book shows you the *kind* of information you can discover from coins and about coins.

Even if you don't actually collect coins but do like to travel or study geography, this book has something to offer you. Coins shown are those used today in other countries, the very coins that pass from hand to hand in daily commerce. If you are a traveler, you can familiarize yourself in advance with the coins you will encounter; and if you are a student, reading about these coins will give you an extra glimpse into life in other lands.

HOW TO GET COINS

How can you get coins for your collection? A good first step is to tell your friends and relatives that you are interested in beginning a collection. You may be surprised at how many people have a few odd coins lying around that they are willing to let you have. If you know people going on a trip outside the country, offer to reimburse them for the cost if they will bring you back a selection of coins in circulation in the countries they visit.

Quite a few countries have agencies that will send coins to collectors abroad. Throughout this book are names of mints, banks and agencies in other lands that have been helpful in supplying collectors with coins of their countries. If no source is given for a particular country, it means that there is no agency and you will have to make private arrangements or get specimens of that country's coins from travelers or coin dealers. The agencies that do supply coins will charge you the face value of the coins you order plus a service charge. Since the coins offered and the instructions for ordering vary from time to time, you should always write to the agency before ordering or sending any money. Tell them that you are a collector and would like a set of coins from their country; ask what coins they can supply, what the cost is, and how you should go about ordering them.

You can also buy coins from coin dealers. You will often find that their prices for current coins are no higher than the cost of ordering direct, if you take the postage and service charge into consideration. Also, in buying from a dealer you get the coins with less delay than waiting for shipment from outside the country. But you may enjoy receiving mail from a foreign country and, when displaying your coins, being able to tell how you went about obtaining them.

Another possible source for coins is the foreign exchange section of the larger banks in your locality.

HOW TO STORE
AND DISPLAY COINS

Once you have decided to start a collection and actually acquire a few coins, you will want to know about the ways of storing and displaying your collection. Many collectors store their coins in two-inch-square envelopes. These are inexpensive and just the right size for most coins. On the outside of the envelope, write all the information you have about the coin inside. The basic facts concerning any coin are:

1. The name of the issuing country
2. The date of issue
3. The denomination
4. The metal
5. Identification of the figures and devices on both sides
6. Translation of the legends if they are in a language other than English
7. The cost and source of each coin

These two-by-two envelopes can be filed in metal or cardboard trays made especially for them. The envelope and tray system is excellent for a general worldwide collection, as it accommodates coins of any size or shape and you can file your collection in any of several ways—alphabetically, geographically, by size or by metal.

Slightly more expensive are the individual cardboard coin holders. With these, you place your coin between two layers of cellophane within a stiff cardboard border. The advantage of this kind of holder is that you can see both sides of your coin without having to remove it from its protective holder. These cardboard holders can be lined up in trays, or they will fit into special album pages which fasten into looseleaf notebooks.

If your collection is limited to just the modern coins of the United States, Britain or Canada, you can use one of the specialized albums with spaces cut to size for a specific coin and imprinted with name and date of the coin that goes into each space. Unfortunately, no printed albums exist for worldwide collections of coins because of the problem of the many different sizes and the fact that no two collections are ever exactly alike. For collections of various-sized coins, you can use one of the blank albums. In these, each page is made up of layers of openings with transparent plastic slides over the top. You slide out a section of plastic, put your coin in place and move the plastic slide back in place.

HANDLING COINS

A few words of caution are in order in regard to handling coins and the advisability of cleaning them. Coins are durable, certainly, but they can be damaged by dropping them, rubbing them together or trying to clean them with strong chemicals. Once a coin comes into your collection, even if it is already somewhat worn, always be careful to see that no further damage is done. Pick up and hold your coins by the edges. Work over a table so that if a coin should fall, it won't drop to the floor. Don't keep your coins loose in a box so that they shake around and scratch each other. Above all, don't try to shine your coins. A little soap and water will usually clean off any accumulated dirt or grime. If this doesn't work, then a paste of baking soda and water can be used on silver coins, a little olive oil on a soft cloth on copper coins. Collectors are very particular about the appearance of their coins, and by "shining them up," you may unknowingly reduce their value.

COIN VALUES

Value, of course, is something that every new collector wants to know about—which coins are valuable and what makes one coin more valuable than another. This book urges you to start your collection with coins that are in use today around the world, coins that you can get for face value or a small extra premium. Eventually you may want to add some older coins, types that are no longer in use. You will have to get your older coins from other collectors or dealers who got them and put them away while they were still available. You will have to pay more for them, too, because the coins of a particular issue go out of circulation; they become scarcer and harder to get and their value goes up accordingly. When many collectors want a particular coin and there are only a few of them available, the price of that coin goes up; this is according to the law of supply and demand.

It follows that the coins you can get easily right now will become scarcer and more valuable as time goes along. Don't expect to make a profit on your coins right away, but there is a good chance that if you hold on to your coins for a few years and protect their condition, they will become worth more than you paid for them.

COIN PUBLICATIONS

You can get information about albums, other collecting accessories and coin prices by visiting a coin dealer or by reading one of the coin publications. Subscribing to a coin paper or magazine is the best way to keep up with the news about coins. In such publications you will find announcements of worldwide new issues as well as interesting stories about coins that are already in circulation. Every issue carries dealers' advertising so you can make contacts if you want to buy coins to fill out your collection. Here are the names of the best-known publications:

Coin World (weekly)
P.O. Box 150
Sidney, Ohio 45365 $6.00 per year

Coins and Medals (monthly)
Link House
Dingwall Avenue
Croydon CR9 2TA, England
                    £1 17s. per year
                    ($4.50 to U.S.A.)

Coins Magazine (monthly)
Iola, Wisconsin 54945 $5.00 per year

Coins, Medals, and Currency (weekly)
2 Arundel Street
London, W.C. 2, England
                    £4 per year
                    ($10.00 to U.S.A.)

Numismatic News (every two weeks)
Iola, Wisconsin 54945 $5.00 per year

Numismatic Scrapbook Magazine
  (monthly)
P.O. Box 150
Sidney, Ohio 45365 $5.00 per year

The Numismatist (monthly)
P.O. Box 2366
Colorado Springs, Colorado 80901
                    $6.00 per year
This is the official publication of the American Numismatic Society. Membership in the organization is open to collectors eleven years of age and over. Write to the organization for details.

Seaby's Coin & Medal Bulletin
  (monthly)
59-65 Great Portland Street
London, W. 1, England
                    17/6 per year
                    ($2.50 to U.S.A.)

World Coins (monthly)
P.O. Box 150
Sidney, Ohio 45365 $5.00 per year

COINS IN CIRCULATION
AROUND THE WORLD

100 cents = 1 dollar

half-dollar	Head of Kennedy.	Rev.° Presidential Seal.
quarter-dollar	Head of Washington.	Rev. Eagle.
1 dime	Head of Roosevelt.	Rev. Torch of Freedom.
5 cents	Head of Jefferson.	Rev. Monticello.
1 cent	Head of Lincoln.	Rev. Lincoln Memorial.

Rev. = reverse.

American coins show portraits of five former Presidents, from the first President, George Washington (1789–97), to John F. Kennedy (1960–63). President Lyndon B. Johnson asked Congress for legislation authorizing a new memorial coin less than three weeks after the assassination of President Kennedy, his predecessor. The Presidential Seal on the half-dollar reverse shows a heraldic eagle with an olive branch, symbol of peace, in its right talon, and a bundle of arrows symbolizing preparedness in its left. The shield on the eagle's breast has thirteen stripes for

23

the original thirteen American colonies that became states. These first states are also represented in the number of olive leaves, berries, arrows, clouds and the stars above the eagle. Around the eagle is a circle of fifty stars, one for each of today's states. The E PLURIBUS UNUM motto that appears on all denominations is Latin for "One out of many" and refers also to the union of the states.

The other twentieth-century President whose portrait is on a coin is Franklin D. Roosevelt (1933–45), who was placed on the dime in 1946, the year following his death. America's wartime leader had the distinction of being the only President elected to serve four terms (a Constitutional amendment now limits Presidents to two four-year terms). The freedom torch on the reverse commemorates Roosevelt's 1941 speech outlining the "four essential human freedoms . . . freedom of speech and expression; freedom of worship; freedom from want; freedom from fear." The dime is equal to 10 cents, the word itself coming from the Latin *decima,* meaning tenth.

U.S. coinage began in 1793 during the administration of George Washington. Some leaders proposed placing Washington's portrait on the new coins, but he rejected the idea as being the practice of monarchs. Thus, George Washington did not appear on a regular issue U.S. coin until 1932, the two hundredth anniversary of his birth. The eagle on the reverse was the design specified in the original coin law of 1792 establishing U.S. coinage. An unbroken series of eagle reverses have appeared on U.S. quarter-dollars.

The 1-cent piece shows the familiar bearded face of Abraham Lincoln (1861–65), who is still revered throughout the world as a symbol of freedom and equality. Lincoln was an inexperienced man with little formal education. Yet, faced with a civil war, Lincoln preserved the Union and abolished slavery. The IN GOD WE TRUST motto now on the obverse of all U.S. coins was first used during Lincoln's term in office. The reverse of the Lincoln cent shows the Lincoln Memorial in Washington, D.C. The name of the denomination also comes from a Latin word, *centum,* meaning hundred. The U.S. cent was the forerunner of all the cents, centavos, centimes, centesimi and centimos in use throughout the world.

Third President Thomas Jefferson (1801–9) is best known as the author of the Declaration of Independence and, during his term of office, for the purchase of the Louisiana Territory from France. Jefferson was also largely responsible for persuading the Continental Congress to establish the decimal coinage system since adopted by most other nations. The reverse of the 5-cent piece shows Monticello, Jefferson's home near Charlottesville, Virginia. Monticello means "little mountain," the name of that part of the Jefferson estate on which the home was built. Noncollectors often wrongly identify the building on the back of the 5-cent piece as the White House, and although there is a certain similarity between the two, the name Monticello is clearly spelled out on the coin itself. Monticello is now preserved as a national shrine.

U.S. dollars are now issued as paper money only, silver dollars last being minted in 1935. Large quantities of dollar-size coins were first struck in Europe in the early 1500s at Joachimsthal (Joachim's Valley) in Bohemia. These coins became popular all over Europe. Called "thalers" from their place of origin, the name changed to "taler," to "daler" and finally to "dollar" by the time it reached the New World. U.S. dimes, quarters and half-dollars were struck on fine silver planchets until 1965. The rising price and shortage of silver have made changes necessary,

Benjamin Franklin half-dollar

and the new half-dollars contain only 40 percent silver, the dimes and quarters none at all.

In addition to the coins being issued now, coins of older design occasionally turn up in circulation. The half-dollar with a portrait of Benjamin Franklin was struck as recently as 1963; and dimes with the winged Liberty head, Indian-buffalo nickels and standing Liberty quarters can also be found. Most of the earlier-design coins still in circulation are badly worn. Well-preserved specimens are scarce and worth looking for as additions to your collection.

For information about coins of the United States, write to:

Officer in Charge, U. S. Assay Office
Numismatic Service
350 Duboce Avenue
San Francisco, California 94102, U.S.A.

100 cents = 1 dollar

1 dollar	Portrait of Queen Elizabeth II with coronet.	Rev. Voyageurs.
50 cents	Same.	Rev. Coat of arms.
25 cents	Same.	Rev. Caribou head.
10 cents	Same.	Rev. Fishing schooner.
5 cents	Same.	Rev. Beaver.
1 cent	Same.	Rev. Maple leaves.

At one time, both France and Great Britain laid claim to parts of Canada. Although the English, under John Cabot, were first to arrive, the French, led by Jacques Cartier, began bartering with the Indians and opened up the profitable fur trade. French traders, often with Indian companions, penetrated deep into the wilderness in fragile birchbark canoes. These early *voyageurs* are represented on the reverse of Canada's silver dollar. In the background are some pine trees and in the sky, the *aurora borealis,* the northern lights. Beavers, whose pelts were the early medium of exchange, are recalled on the 5-cent piece reverse.

27

Britain ultimately won control of all of Canada, and coins of the mother country were used until 1858, the year Canada began its own distinctive coinage based on the American system of cents and dollars rather than British pounds. Today, Canada is a completely self-governing member of the British Commonwealth. Queen Elizabeth is nominally represented in Canada by a governor general, and her portrait appears on the obverse of the entire coin series.

Canada's half-dollar reverse shows the Canadian coat of arms, composed of the emblems of Canada and the four countries from which her population has mainly come. In the upper left quarter of the shield are the three lions of England; in the upper right, the Scottish lion. At center left is the harp of Ireland and at right, the three fleurs-de-lis (lilies) of France. In the base are three maple leaves, the emblem of Canada. The scroll below the shield carries the motto A MARI USQUE AD MARE, "From sea to sea." The maple-leaf motif also dominates the reverse of the 1-cent piece.

On the reverse of a quarter-dollar is the head of a caribou, a North American reindeer. Finally, the 10-cent piece shows a fishing schooner under sail. Although it is not officially designated as any particular ship, the craft shown resembles the *Bluenose,* a famous Nova Scotian racing ship that was later pictured on a Canadian postage stamp.

The hundredth anniversary of Canada's status as a Dominion in 1967 was honored by the introduction of new designs for all the coins. The regular designs were resumed in 1968, and pure nickel replaced silver in the planchets for the dollar, half-dollar, quarter-dollar, and 10-cent piece.

For information about coins of Canada, write to:

Coins Uncirculated
P.O. Box 470
Ottawa, Ontario, Canada

100 centavos = 1 peso

1 peso	Eagle on cactus.	Rev. Bust of Morelos.
50 centavos	Same.	Rev. Head of Cuauhtemoc.
25 centavos	Same.	Rev. Portrait of Madero.
10 centavos	Same.	Rev. Bust of Juarez.
5 centavos	Same.	Rev. Bust of Doña Josefa.
1 centavo	Same.	Rev. Wheat stalk.

One side of every Mexican coin features an eagle holding a serpent in its beak. This emblem is the coat of arms of Mexico and derives from an old Aztec legend. According to the legend, the Aztecs' gods told them that they should settle at the place where they would find an eagle sitting on a cactus plant on a stone in the water and tearing a serpent apart with its beak and claws. The Aztecs are said to have seen this very sight at Lake Texcoco, where they established their city of Tenochtitlán, later known as Mexico City.

On the other side of her coins, Mexico honors national heroes. The last emperor of the Aztecs, called Cuauhtemoc (1495–1525), is shown on the 50-centavo piece. Cuauhtemoc led the

Indians' battle against the Spanish Conquistadores but was eventually defeated and captured. The Spaniards tried to discover the hiding place of the Aztecs' gold, but even under torture Cuauhtemoc refused to reveal the whereabouts of the hidden treasure, which remains lost to this day.

The 1-peso coin (peso is Spanish for weight) carries the portrait of José María Morelos y Pavón (1765–1815), a humble parish priest who was a leader in the fight for Mexican independence from Spain. Morelos suffered from constant headaches and his coin portraits show him with a handkerchief tied around his head, a practice he felt relieved him from pain.

Another hero of this revolution, a lady, Josefa Ortiz de Dominguez (d. 1829) appears on the 5-centavo piece. Doña Josefa was the wife of the Spanish governor but she was sympathetic to the independence movement. By warning the rebel leaders of the governor's plans, she saved them from danger but was arrested herself. She was forced to stand trial and was later imprisoned.

Benito Juárez (1806–72), on the 10-centavo piece, was a full-blooded Zapotec Indian who was three time elected President of the Mexican republic. Juárez led the opposition to the Austrian Archduke Maximilian, who, with the help of French troops, set up a Mexican empire during the 1860's.

The 25-cent coin shows Francisco I. Madero (1873–1913), President from 1911 to 1913. Madero was largely responsible for ending the dictatorial regime of Porfirio Díaz. Unable to carry out his promised reforms he was taken into custody and executed. The 1-centavo coin showing three sheaves of wheat is still being minted but has such a small value that it is never seen in actual circulation. Many of these coins are used in making jewelry, especially bracelets, for sale to tourists.

The denominations of the Mexican coins are written in Spanish: *uno* for one, *cinco* for five, *diez* for ten, *veinticinco* for twenty-five, and *cincuenta* for fifty. Collectors who study their coins carefully can learn many words in foreign languages.

100 cents = 1 dollar

5 dollars	Portrait of Queen Elizabeth II.	Rev. Coat of arms.
2 dollars	Same.	Rev. Flamingos.
1 dollar	Same.	Rev. Conch shell.
50 cents	Same.	Rev. Leaping marlin.
25 cents	Same.	Rev. Sailing sloop.

15 cents	Portrait of Queen Elizabeth II.	Rev. Hibiscus blossom (square planchet).
10 cents	Same.	Rev. Bonefish and seaweed (scalloped planchet).
5 cents	Same.	Rev. Pineapple.
1 cent	Same.	Rev. Starfish.

The historic first landing of Columbus on October 12, 1492, took place on one of the 700 islands making up the Bahamas group. Originally Spanish, the islands were taken over by the British in 1783. The capital city and favorite vacation spot is Nassau on New Providence Island.

Until 1966, regular English coins were in circulation, but the islands have now switched to a decimal coinage of their own. The obverses of all the new coins show the portrait of Queen Elizabeth of Great Britain. The reverse of the 5-dollar coin shows the badge of the islands, a royal crown with three sailing ships below and the motto EXPULSIS PIRATIS RESTITUTA COMMERCIA, "Commerce restored by the defeat of the pirates." The significance of the motto is that during the seventeenth century the islands were used as a base by pirates who were finally expelled when the island came under Crown government in 1717. The reverses of the other eight coins feature objects associated with the islands.

Since tourism is the main industry of the Bahamas, many of the attractive new coins will undoubtedly be carried away as souvenirs. Nine different values seem like more coins than necessary to make change, but the 5-dollar and 2-dollar pieces are not expected to circulate at all, and the 1-dollar and 50-cent coins may have only limited use, since paper money is also being issued in these denominations.

For information about coins of the Bahamas, write to:

The Treasury
P.O. Box 557
Nassau, Bahamas

12 pence = 1 shilling
5 shillings = 1 crown

1 crown   Crowned head of Queen Elizabeth II.   Rev. Coat of arms.

The Bermudas are a group of British islands in the western North Atlantic. The capital city and main tourist center is Hamilton, on Bermuda Island. The islands are named after Juan de Bermudez, a Spanish sea captain who discovered them in 1503. The islands were occupied by the British in 1609 by Admiral Sir George Somers, whose ship, *Sea Venture,* was wrecked on an offshore reef.

Bermuda circulates regular English coins but has issued two special crown pieces, the latter in 1964. The reverse of this coin shows the island's badge, a seated facing lion holding a shield bearing the wreck of the *Sea Venture.* The scroll below reads QUO FATA PERUNT, "Where the Fates lead us."

The special crowns were not actually put into circulation, but banks in Bermuda did allow one coin per customer at face value.

100 cents = 1 dollar

1 dollar	Jamaican coat of arms.	Rev. Sir Alexander Bustamante.
25 cents	Same.	Rev. Swallowtail hummingbird.
20 cents	Same.	Rev. Tree (blue mahoe).
10 cents	Same.	Rev. Tree (lignum vitae).
5 cents	Same.	Rev. Crocodile.
1 cent	Same.	Rev. Ackee plant.

Columbus landed at Jamaica on his second and fourth trans-Atlantic voyages in 1494 and 1503. Henry Morgan, the famed privateer, used the old capital city of Port Royal as his base. This intriguing old association with pirates is one of Jamaica's lures as a modern tourist attraction.

Until 1969, Jamaicans used regular English coins except for the two lowest denominations, the penny and the halfpenny, which carried distinctive designs. In September, 1969, Jamaica adopted a decimal currency with 100 cents to the dollar. The six new decimal coins all have the Jamaican shield of arms—a cross with five pineapples, supported by a West Indian woman with a basket of fruit and flowers and by a West Indian warrior holding a bow. The crest above the shield is an alligator on a log. The scroll at the bottom reads OUT OF MANY, ONE PEOPLE.

The new 1-dollar coin shows Sir Alexander Bustamante, Jamaica's first prime minister, who served from 1962 until 1967. The reverses of the rest of the coins show plants and animals native to the island.

100 cents = 1 guilder

2 1/2 gulden	Head of Queen Juliana.	Rev. Coat of arms.
1 guilder	Same.	Same.
1/4 guilder	Same.	Same.
1/10 guilder	Same.	Same.
5 cents	Orange branch.	Rev. Value (square planchet).
2 1/2 cents	Lion.	Rev. Value.
1 cent	Same.	Same.

The islands of the Netherlands Antilles, stopping points for many steamships and airlines, have been drawing an increasing number of tourists. The main islands are Curaçao, Aruba and St. Eustatius.

The coins in use in the Antilles show the head of the Netherlands' queen on the obverse of the higher denominations. The reverses show the ancestral coat of arms of Queen Juliana's royal house of Orange-Nassau—dating from the Middle Ages—a

35

crowned rampant lion holding a sword in one paw, a sheaf of arrows in the other. The 5-cent coin shows an orange branch, an allusion to the name of the royal line, but possibly also to a well-known liqueur flavored with the dried peel of bitter oranges and called Curaçao after its place of origin.

For information about coins of the Netherlands Antilles, write to:

Hollandsche Bank—Unie N.V.
Breeddstraat No. 1
Willemstad, Curaçao

100 cents = 1 gourde

20 centimes	Head of President Duvalier.	Rev. Coat of arms.
10 centimes	Same.	Same.

The island of Hispaniola was originally divided between the French in the western portion and the Spanish in the eastern. The French area declared itself an independent empire in 1804, taking the name Haiti. A republic since 1859, French has remained the official language of Haiti, and on the reverse of Haiti's coins is the well-known legend LIBERTE, EGALITE, FRATERNITE, "Liberty, equality, brotherhood." The device on the reverse is the national coat of arms, a palm tree surmounted by a Cap of Liberty, with a drum in front and at each side three flags, three rifles, a cannon and a pile of cannon balls. The ribbon below carries the motto L'UNION FAIT LA FORCE, "Union makes strength."

The obverse of Haiti's coinage shows the portrait of the current president, an honor usually bestowed only on royalty or deceased national heroes.

The monetary unit, the gourde, has not been struck as a coin since the last century. This unusual name for a coin denomination derives from the island custom of using actual gourds (*gourde* in French) as a measure of value in the days of barter trading.

For information about coins of Haiti, write to:

> Banque Nationale de la Republique d'Haiti
> Head Office, Rue Americaine & Rue Fereu
> Port-au-Prince, Haiti

37

DOMINICAN REPUBLIC

100 centavos = 1 peso

50 centavos	Liberty head with feather head-dress (12 1/2 gramos on right side of coins stands for weight)	Rev. Coat of arms.
25 centavos	Same.	Same.
10 centavos	Same.	Same.
5 centavos	Same.	Same.
1 centavo	Palm tree.	Same.

The eastern (Spanish) portion of the island of Hispaniola declared itself an independent republic in 1844, taking the name Dominican Republic. Dominican coinage began in 1891, and recent coins show the same motifs as the original issues. On the obverse is a female personification of Liberty wearing a feathered Indian headdress with LIBERTAD (Liberty) on the band. The design is reminiscent of the familiar U.S. Indian-head cent that was being issued at the time, and, in fact, Liberty-head designs have been popular throughout all of Latin America. The reverse shows the national arms, a shield bearing a white cross with an open Book of the Gospels, a small cross above, all surrounded by a trophy of lances and flags. The motto on the label above, DIOS, PATRIA, LIBERTAD, "God, country, liberty," was chosen by Juan Pablo Duarte, who led the movement of independence from the neighboring state of Haiti. The lowest value, the 1 centavo, shows a palm tree, a familiar sight in the warm climate of the island, on the obverse.

For information about coins of the Dominican Republic, write to:

Banco Central de Santo Domingo
Santo Domingo, Dominican Republic

NICARAGUA

100 centavos = 1 cordoba

50 centavos	Bust of Córdoba.	Rev. Sun and five mountain peaks.
25 centavos	Same.	Same.
10 centavos	Same.	Same.
5 centavos	Same.	Same.

Central America is a narrow thousand-mile-long land bridge connecting the North and South American continents. Under Spanish rule, this area was known as the Captaincy General of Guatemala, and was divided into the provinces of Guatemala, Costa Rica, El Salvador, Nicaragua and Honduras. Winning their independence from Spain in 1821, the five provinces joined together to form the Central American Republic. This union dissolved into independent states after a few years, but it is still recalled on the modern coins of Nicaragua, which carry on the reverse side a design taken from the national coat of arms. The five mountain peaks represent the original members of the Central American Republic. The motto EN DIOS CONFIAMOS is the Spanish version of the U.S. coin motto, "In God we trust."

The obverse of the Nicaragua coin series shows the bust of Francisco Hernández de Córdoba (1475–1526) decked out in a ruffled collar, the court dress of his day. Córdoba led the forces that occupied Nicaragua, and in 1524 he founded its cities of León and Granada. After bringing the area under Spanish control, Córdoba began planning to set up an independent state

40

with himself as governor; but his superiors, learning of the plot, had Córdoba imprisoned. Convicted of treason, he was beheaded in June 1526.

The monetary unit specified on the coins is the cordoba, named for the conqueror. A coin of this denomination was struck just once, in 1912, and the unit is now issued only as paper money.

For information about coins of Nicaragua, write to:

Banco Central de Nicaragua
Managua, Nicaragua

100 centesimos = 1 balboa

1 balboa	Bust of Balboa.	Rev. Female figure, coat of arms.
1/2 balboa	Same.	Rev. Coat of arms.
1/4 balboa	Same.	Same.
1/10 balboa	Same.	Same.
5 centesimos	Coat of arms.	Rev. Value.
1 centesimo	Head of Urraca.	Same.

Panama came into being as a sovereign nation in 1903. Formerly a department of Colombia, the Panamanians were disappointed over Colombia's rejection of a U.S. Canal treaty. They successfully revolted and quickly made their own treaty with the U.S. The Canal's history figures prominently in the coat of arms displayed on the balboa, the one-half (*medio*) balboa and the five centesimos coins. The center band shows the isthmus of Panama with the moon at one side, a rising sun at the other. The upper quarterings show a crossed rifle and sword and a crossed shovel and rake. The lower quarterings show a cornucopia and a winged wheel. The motto is PRO MUNDI BENEFICIO, "For the benefit of the world."

The obverse of the higher value coins shows an armored bust of Vasco Núñez de Balboa (1475–1519), the first European to cross the isthmus and see the Pacific Ocean, which he called the South Sea (*El Mar del Sur*), claiming it for the Spanish crown. Although Balboa is known to have dealt fairly with the Indians and always looked after the welfare of his own men, he was falsely accused of treason by Governor Pedrarias and was beheaded in January 1517. Panama has named a city and its monetary unit after the explorer.

While nearly everyone has heard of the feats of Balboa and the other Spanish explorers, very little is known about the people they conquered. On its 1-centesimo coin, Panama has honored Urraca, an Indian chief who led the tribes against the Spanish Conquistadores. Although Urraca was captured, he escaped and waged warfare for nine years. He finally died lamenting on his deathbed his inability to drive out the invaders.

Panama uses U.S. paper money, and the balboa and the dollar are always at par.

100 centavos = 1 quetzal

50 centavos	Coat of arms.	Rev. White nun orchid.
25 centavos	Same.	Rev. Quiche Indian woman.
10 centavos	Same.	Rev. Quiriga column.
5 centavos	Same.	Rev. Ceiba tree.
1 centavo	Same.	Rev. Fray Bartolomé.

The land that is now Guatemala was once the center of the great Maya-Quiche civilization. The ancient Mayans developed a 365–day calendar; their astronomers had calculated the length of the year more accurately than those who formulated the Julian calendar used in England until the mid-eighteenth century. Archaeologists learned about this accomplishment by studying hieroglyphic-like Mayan carvings, as on the monolith from the excavation at Quiriga, shown on the 10-centavo piece. Guatemala's population today is still about 60 percent pure Indian, many of whom still prefer to wear the traditional garb as shown on the 25-centavo coin. In 1524 Spanish Conquistadores under Pedro de Alvarado occupied this land. During the days of Spanish colonial rule, the Indian population was often oppressed and even enslaved. One person who worked hard to improve the lot of the Indians was Fray Bartolomé de Las Casas (shown on the 1-centavo coin) (1474–1566), the first priest ordained in the New World, who has been called the Apostle of the Indies.

A Spanish mint in Guatemala began striking coins as early as 1733. The original Guatemala mint mark was "G." An earthquake destroyed Guatemala City in 1773, and upon rebuilding in 1776, it was called New Guatemala and the mint mark became "NG." Guatemala won its independence from Spain in 1821, and today has the only Central American mint in operation.

The obverses of the Guatemala coin series bear the national arms, a scroll inscribed LIBERTAD 15 DE SEPTEMBRE 1821, surmounted by a quetzal, behind which are crossed rifles and two crossed swords surrounded by a wreath of laurel. The quetzal is a small bird with long tail plumes that reach a length of three and a half feet. The tail feathers were worn as headdresses by the Mayan priests and nobles, and thus became a symbol of the nation. The quetzal is also symbolic of freedom, as it was once believed it would die in captivity. The Guatemalan monetary unit is also named for this bird, but the 1-quetzal coin was struck just once, in 1925, and specimens of this issue are very rare.

The remaining two denominations show on the reverse the national flower, the white nun orchid (*Monja blanca* in Spanish), and a ceiba or silk cotton tree with the legend LIBRE CREZCA FECUNDO, "Free, growing, fruitful." The tree is native to the moist American tropics and is one of the largest in the forest. Its fruit is a source of kapok used for life jackets and mattress stuffing.

For information about coins of Guatemala, write to:

Banco de Guatemala
Guatemala, Central America

EL SALVADOR

100 centavos = 1 colon

50 centavos	Head of Morazan.	Rev. Value.
25 centavos	Same.	Same.
10 centavos	Same.	Same.
5 centavos	Same.	Same.
1 centavo	Same.	Same.

The smallest of the Central American republics, El Salvador honors Francisco Morazán (1799–1842) on its coins. From 1830 until 1840, Morazán was president of the Central American Confederation of which El Salvador was a member. El Salvador declared its independence in 1841 but has since made several attempts to reestablish the political union of the Central American republics.

El Salvador's monetary unit is the colon, named for Christopher Columbus (Cristóbal Colón in Spanish).

100 centimos = 1 colon

2 colones	Coat of arms.	Rev. Value.
1 colon	Same.	Same.
50 centimos	Same.	Same.
25 centimos	Same.	Same.
10 centimos	Same.	Same.
5 centimos	Same.	Same.

Costa Rica, as did El Salvador, named its coin unit the colon in honor of Columbus. The name of the country, which in Spanish means "rich coast," is attributed to Columbus, who reported seeing the native Indians wearing gold ornaments. Costa Rica was also a member of the Central American Federation during the last century, a fact marked by the five stars in the coat of arms shown on the obverse of the current coinage. The main device, three volcanoes separating two oceans, each with a sailing ship, recalls Costa Rica's location between the Atlantic and Pacific Oceans.

HONDURAS

100 centavos = 1 lempira

50 centavos	Coat of arms.	Rev. Head of Lempira.
20 centavos	Same.	Same.
10 centavos	Same.	Rev. Value.
5 centavos	Same.	Same.
2 centavos	Same.	Same.
1 centavo	Same.	Same.

Honduras' name is also attributed to Columbus, who landed here in 1502 on his fourth voyage. The name means "depths" and comes from the deep water he found off the Caribbean coast. Spain's conquest of Honduras was not easy and was only accomplished through violence and treachery. Perhaps the most invincible Indian the Spanish came up against in the New World was Lempira, whose name means "Lord of the Mountains." Lempira gathered an army of thirty thousand Indians and is reputed to have himself killed more than a hundred of the enemy. Lempira was tricked into a peace conference and murdered. Honduras has honored this early hero by placing his portrait on the highest denomination coins and naming the monetary unit the lempira.

The obverses show the national coat of arms, whose main device is a pyramid symbolizing equality and justice. The arched door (rainbow) is for hope; the two towers stand for sovereignty and independence.

100 cents = 1 dollar

50 cents	Crowned head of Queen Elizabeth II.	Rev. Value.
25 cents	Same.	Same.
10 cents	Same.	Same.
5 cents	Same.	Same.
1 cent	Same. (Scalloped-edge planchet.)	Same.

British Honduras is the only colony in Central America. The area was settled by the British, who founded Belize, the capital city, during the mid-seventeenth century. England's claim to the small territory was disputed by Spain in colonial times and by Guatemala in recent years. British Honduras has had a regular issue of distinctive coins since 1885, all bearing the portrait of the current English sovereign.

49

BRAZIL

100 centavos = 1 cruzeiro

2 cruzeiros	Star.	Rev. Value.
1 cruzeiro	Same.	Same.
50 centavos	Same.	Same.
20 centavos	Same.	Same.
10 centavos	Same.	Same.

Brazil, the largest country in South America, occupies nearly half of the continent. Settled by the Portuguese as *Terra da Vera Cruz* (Land of the True Cross) the nation's language and heritage are Portuguese, in contrast to the Spanish tradition of the rest of South America. A treaty made in 1494, only two years after Columbus' discovery of America, delineated the area to be settled by Spain and by Portugal. Brazil's modern name comes from brazilwood, which early traders sought for its value as a source of coloring matter for dye.

In recent years Brazil has suffered a runaway inflation that has undermined her currency. The value of the cruzeiro has dropped to a fraction of a cent, and the only currency now in daily circulation is paper money.

The last Brazilian coins actually to circulate showed the nation's coat of arms on the obverse—a large five-pointed star with a center circle of twenty smaller stars representing Brazil's states. The five center stars form the Southern Cross constellation, a reminder that Brazil lies almost entirely below the equator. The leaves behind the stars are from coffee and tobacco plants, two of Brazil's most important products.

25 pesos	Replica of obverse and reverse of early coin.	
10 pesos	Gaucho on horseback.	Rev. Value.
5 pesos	Sailing ship.	Same.

Argentina, which is today the largest Spanish-speaking country in the world, was the first of Spain's American possessions to gain independence. She began her own coinage in 1813, and a reproduction of the first coin type is shown on the modern 25-peso coin with the inscription PRIMERA MONEDA PATRIA, "First coin of the country." The coin reproduced is an 1813 8-reales piece showing on the obverse the original coat of arms, a cap of liberty and two clasped hands, the symbol of brotherhood and unity. The legend reads UNION Y LIBERTAD, "Union and liberty." The reverse legend reads PROVINCIAS DEL RIO DE LA PLATA, "Provinces of the La Plata [silver] River," Argentina's original name. In the center is a radiate sun with the human features of eyes, nose and mouth, a device with roots in the ancient Inca practice of sun worship. This Inca emblem was chosen to recall an earlier time of independence before the arrival of the Spaniards.

Argentina's 10-peso coin shows a gaucho, one of the cowboys of the South American pampas (plains) famous for their horsemanship and skill with the lasso and bola (a rope with weights at the end for entangling an animal's feet). The gauchos wear a picturesque outfit: a wide-brimmed hat, bright shirt, loose-fitting trousers and high boots. The 5-peso coin shows the Argentine sailing ship, the frigate *Presidente Sarmiento,* a former navy school ship.

100 centesimos = 1 peso

1 peso	Head of Artigas.	Rev. Coat of arms.
50 centesimos	Same.	Same.
25 centesimos	Same.	Same.
10 centesimos	Same.	Rev. Value.
5 centesimos	Same.	Same.
2 centesimos	Same.	Same.

Uruguay, the smallest South American republic, serves as a buffer state between Brazil and Argentina, the largest South American nations. The official name of the nation as shown on its coins, is REPUBLICA ORIENTAL DEL URUGUAY, "Republic east of the Uruguay," referring to its location on the eastern side of the Uruguay River, which separates it from Argentina.

On the obverse of its coins, Uruguay honors José Gervasio Artigas, the leader of the nation's war for independence that began in 1810. During colonial times Uruguay was a part of the Spanish viceroyalty centered in Argentina. Artigas not only joined the revolt of Buenos Aires against Spain, he succeeded in breaking Uruguay off from Argentina.

The reverse of the higher denomination coins shows Uruguay's coat of arms. In the upper quarters are scales representing justice and a mountain as an emblem of strength. In the lower quarters are an untamed horse symbolizing liberty and an ox for cattle raising, the chief industry. The sun at the top of the shield is a reminder of the nation's former association with Argentina.

COLOMBIA

100 centavos = 1 peso

50 centavos	Head of Bolívar.	Rev. Coat of arms.
20 centavos	Same.	Same.
10 centavos	Indian head.	Same.
2 centavos	Liberty head.	Rev. Value.

Like several other South American nations, Colombia honors a revolutionary patriot on her coins—Simón Bolívar, "El Libertador." Although Bolívar was the son of aristocratic parents, he devoted his life to freeing South America from Spanish rule. He led campaigns in Venezuela, Ecuador and Peru as well as in Colombia, the latter called New Granada by the Spanish. His victories in battle proved Bolívar's ability as a great soldier, although he was not able to achieve his dream of uniting South America into one country.

The reverses of the higher value coins show the Colombian coat of arms. In the top band is a pomegranate between two cornucopiae. The pomegranate was the badge of the old Spanish kingdom of Granada and can be seen today also in the coat of arms on Spanish coins. The middle band shows a liberty cap on a pole and, at the bottom, is the isthmus of Panama with a sailing ship on each side (Panama was a province of Colombia until 1903).

54

100 centimos = 1 bolivar

2 bolivares	Head of Bolívar.	Rev. Coat of arms.
1 bolivar	Same.	Same.
50 centimos	Same.	Same.
25 centimos	Same.	Same.
12 1/2 centimos	Coat of arms.	Rev. Value.
5 centimos	Same.	Same.

Venezuela, like Colombia, shows Simón Bolívar on its coins with the nation's coat of arms on the reverse. This is an appropriate honor since "El Libertador" was born in Caracas, Venezuela, and secured Venezuelan as well as Colombian independence by his victory over the Spanish forces. For a time he was the president of Greater Colombia, a short-lived union of Venezuela and Colombia. Throughout South America Bolívar is considered the greatest hero in Latin American history.

On the shield of arms are a sheaf of corn (unity and fertility), two flags with swords (a victory trophy), and a wild horse (liberty).

The unusual 12½-centimos denomination (one eighth of a bolivar) is a holdover from colonial days when the large dollar-size coin was divided into 8 reales.

For information about coins of Venezuela, write to:

Banco Centrale de Venezuela
Caracas, Venezuela

55

100 centavos = 1 sucre

1 sucre	Head of Sucre.	Rev. Coat of arms.
50 centavos	Coat of arms.	Rev. Value.
20 centavos	Same.	Same.
10 centavos	Same.	Same.
5 centavos	Same.	Same.

Antonio José de Sucre, another of South America's patriots, became a leader of the insurgent forces in Quito fighting against the Spanish viceroy. Quito, the capital city of modern Ecuador, lies almost on the equator, which does pass right through the country and gives it its name as shown on the coins, REPUBLICA DEL ECUADOR, "Republic of the Equator."

The coat of arms which appears on all denominations shows a view of the snowcapped Andean peak Mt. Chimborazo, a twenty-thousand-foot volcanic mountain, with a river and steamship in the foreground. The steamship commemorates the fact that the first oceangoing steamer on the west coast of South America was built in Ecuador. Above the shield is a condor, a bird found in the high peaks of the Andes Mountains.

100 centesimos = 1 escudo

10 centesimos	Flying condor.	Rev. Value.
5 centesimos	Same.	Same.
2 centesimos	Same.	Same.
1 centesimo	Same.	Same.
half centesimo	Same.	Same.

Ecuador's neighbor to the south, the Republic of Chile, uses a flying condor as the main design for its coins. The condor is said to be the largest flying bird, with a wingspan of up to ten feet. Condors live near the peaks of high mountains such as are found in the Andes that run along the Chile-Argentina border.

Chile is a strangely shaped country, its territory stretching for 2,600 miles along the Pacific coast in a narrow strip with an average width of only 110 miles. The nation's capital is the city of Santiago, where the mint is located. In fact, a mint was established in Santiago as long ago as 1743 while the country was still under Spanish rule. You can see the mint mark of Santiago, S, just below the date on the reverse of the coin illustrated.

PARAGUAY

100 centimos = 1 guarani

50 centimos	Lion.	Rev. Value (scalloped-edge planchet).
25 centimos	Same.	Same.
15 centimos	Same.	Same.
10 centimos	Same.	Same.

The coins of Paraguay all share the same design, a seated lion guarding a staff with a Cap of Liberty on top. In the field is the motto PAZ Y JUSTICIA, "Peace and justice." The design, taken from the national treasury seal, was used on Paraguay's first coins struck in 1845, and it has been repeated often since then. Paraguay's coins are unusual in that all issues since 1953 have been struck on scalloped planchets. The scalloped planchets are decorative but, in addition, serve the practical purpose of being difficult to counterfeit.

100 centavos = 1 sol

1 sol	Coat of arms.	Rev. Llama.
half sol	Same.	Same.
25 centavos	Same.	Rev. Cantuta flower.
10 centavos	Same.	Same.
5 centavos	Same.	Same.

Peru has the grandest history of all the South American countries, having been first the center of the great Inca empire, and later the seat of Spanish rule over most of the continent. The mines of Potosí (now in territory belonging to Bolivia) were the source of immense quantities of gold and silver. Mints went into operation at Lima in 1568 and at Potosí in 1575.

The obverses of the Peruvian coins show the nation's coat of arms, which symbolizes the country's natural riches—fauna, flora, and minerals. At the top are a llama and a cinchona tree; at the bottom, a horn-of-plenty pouring out coins. The reverse of the larger-denomination coins has a llama, which is used as a beast of burden throughout the country.

BOLIVIA

10 bolivianos = 1 bolivar

10 bolivianos	Head of Bolívar.	Rev. Value.
5 bolivianos	Coat of arms.	Same.
1 boliviano	Same.	Same.

The territory that is now Bolivia was part of Peru during Spanish colonial days. Simón Bolívar, the great South American liberator, also led Peru's campaign for independence and was responsible for establishing the area called Upper Peru as a separate nation. In gratitude, the people renamed this new country the Republic of Bolivia. Today the monetary unit as well is named for Bolívar and his portrait is shown on the highest value coin.

The lower value coins display the Bolivian coat of arms—an oval shield showing the mountain of Potosí (mineral riches), an alpaca (wool production), and a breadfruit tree and a sheaf of corn (agriculture and fertility).

After the discovery of silver at Potosí in 1545, tons of silver bars and coins were sent back to Spain. Bolivia's economy is still based on the output of its mines, but despite the mineral wealth of the country, only base metal is used for its coins. Because of severe inflation, coins have all but disappeared from circulation, and paper money has taken their place.

$$12 \text{ pence } = 1 \text{ shilling}$$
$$5 \text{ shillings } = 1 \text{ crown}$$
$$4 \text{ crowns } = 1 \text{ pound}$$

half crown	Head of Queen Elizabeth II.	Rev. Coat of arms.
2 shillings	Same.	Rev. Double rose.
1 shilling	Same.	Rev. English lions.
1 shilling	Same.	Rev. Scottish lion.
6 pence	Same.	Rev. Garland of rose, thistle, shamrock and leek.
3 pence	Same.	Rev. Chained portcullis (twelve-sided planchet).
1 penny	Same.	Rev. Britannia.
halfpenny	Same.	Rev. The *Golden Hind.*

61

Coinage of Great Britain dates back at least twenty centuries to a form of "ring money" used by the ancient Celtic tribes. Coins were first produced in quantity during the four centuries (A.D. 43–401) that Britain was a province of the Roman Empire. Britain's penny is descended from the denarius of the Romans, and in fact the abbreviation "d" is used today to represent "penny." Britain's monetary system of 12 pence to the shilling and 20 shillings to the pound (yielding 240 pence to the pound) is a source of confusion to foreigners, most of whom are accustomed to coinages based on 10's and 100's.

British coins all show the head of the reigning monarch, so most of the coins in circulation carry the portrait of Queen Elizabeth II. Coins of her father, George VI, however, are still plentiful, although from the sixpence up they are mostly dated after 1946 when silver was discontinued as a coinage metal. The older silver coins were melted down to pay off Lend-Lease loans. The bronze pennies have not changed in size or alloy since 1860, and pennies and halfpennies even from the reign of Queen Victoria (1837–1901) occasionally turn up in circulation.

The reverse of the half crown shows the royal arms and cipher, ER (Elizabeth Regina). The shield shows the three lions of England in the first and fourth quarters, the rampant Scottish lion in the second and the harp of Ireland in the third. The name florin, taken from the Latin word for flower, was first applied to an early Italian coin with a lily as the main feature of its design.

The modern coin carries on the floral tradition with a large English double rose surrounded by Irish shamrocks and Scottish thistles. The halfpenny reverse shows Sir Francis Drake's ship, the *Golden Hind,* the first English vessel to circumnavigate the globe.

One additional denomination, the crown, is issued from time to time in limited quantity to celebrate special occasions. The last issue, in 1965, was to honor Sir Winston Churchill, Britain's wartime prime minister.

Many of Britain's former colonies and the Commonwealth nations have already switched to decimal coinage systems. Britain itself will decimalize in 1971, a step that has been under consideration now for more than a century. The pound will remain the major unit of currency, but it will be divided into 100 pence (called newpence). The first of the new decimal coins, the 5-newpence piece (equivalent to the shilling) and the 10-newpence piece (equivalent to the florin) are already in use, circulating side by side with the older coins.

12 pence = 1 shilling
5 shillings = 1 crown

half crown	Harp.	Rev. Horse.
1 florin	Same.	Rev. Salmon.
(2 shillings)		
1 shilling	Same.	Rev. Bull.
6 pence	Same.	Rev. Wolfhound.
3 pence	Same.	Rev. Hare.
1 penny	Same.	Rev. Hen and chicks.
halfpenny	Same.	Rev. Sow and piglets.
1 farthing	Same.	Rev. Woodcock.

One side of each of Ireland's coins shows a harp, a device first used on Irish coins during the reign of Henry VIII (1509–47), the first of the English kings to take the title "King of Ireland." The triangular harp as depicted on the coins was introduced to the island by Viking invaders, and harp playing was very popular

64

in Ireland during the Middle Ages. The Irish people are known for their fondness for music, so it is not surprising that the harp came to be used as an emblem of the country. You can also see this harp in the coat of arms on the reverse of the current British half crown, although only the northern part of Ireland remains as part of the United Kingdom.

The southern counties won their independence from Britain in 1922 and began issuing distinctive coins in 1928. Except for slight modifications in the legend, the original bird, fish and animal designs are still being issued today, so a visitor to Ireland (Eire) can easily assemble a complete set of the nation's coinage from circulation. Their designs have made the Irish coins popular with collectors. Besides being attractive, they show some of the things of which the Irish are especially proud—their fine horses, cattle and dogs; hunting and fishing, represented by a lively salmon and a woodcock; and the new wealth of the land as shown by its domestic animals.

Ireland's coinage plans call for decimalization in early 1971. Ireland's six new decimal coins (50, 10, 5, and 2 newpence, and 1 and ½ newpenny) are to be of the same size, shape, and metallic content as their British equivalents but will retain distinctive Irish designs.

For information about the coins of Ireland, write to:

Central Bank of Ireland
Dublin, Ireland

CHANNEL ISLANDS

GUERNSEY

8 doubles = 1 penny

3 pence	Coat of arms.	Rev. Guernsey cow.
8 doubles	Same.	Rev. Lilies.
4 doubles	Same.	Rev. Lily.

JERSEY

1/4 shilling	Crowned head of Queen Elizabeth II.	Rev. Coat of arms.
1/12 shilling	Same.	Same.

The Channel Islands are located in the English Channel within sight of the French coast, in the waters between the French provinces of Brittany and Normandy. They have become popular holiday spots for Britons, but are best known to the rest of the world through the two breeds of cattle, Guernsey and Jersey, which originated on and are named for the two principal islands.

The islands have belonged to the British Crown since the time of the Norman conquest and are the last remnants of the Duchy of Normandy. The coats of arms are the same as England's, three lions *passant guardant* (walking with the forepaw raised, the face turned toward the viewer), as shown on the British half crown and "English" shilling. Guernsey's coat of arms has a sprig of laurel above it, which differentiates it from Jersey's.

For centuries the official currency of the Channel Islands was French. An old French coin called a double tournois (from the French city of Tours) was widely circulated in the islands. When special British lower value coins replaced the French during the nineteenth century, the "double" was adopted as the unit of coinage for Guernsey. The 3-pence denomination was introduced in 1956 and shows one of the Guernsey cows. The Guernsey coins are unusual as, unlike the other British colonies and dependencies, they bear no likeness of or reference to the reigning British monarch.

French coins also circulated on Jersey until 1834; and to equal the coins being replaced, the Jersey shilling was divided into thirteen pence rather than twelve as in England. The first coins were given the unusual denomination of one thirteenth of a shilling. When the values were later brought into line with the British, the penny-size coin was inscribed as it is today, ONE TWELFTH OF A SHILLING. The ONE FOURTH OF A SHILLING coin is, of course, the same value as the British 3 pence. This situation of two names for the same thing can be seen on U.S. and

Canadian coins. In Canada, coins are inscribed "25 cents" and "50 cents," while in the United States the equivalent coins read "quarter dollar" and "half dollar."

For information about the coins of the Channel Islands, write to:

The States Treasury, Royal Square
St. Helier, Jersey, C.I., Great Britain

100 centimes = 1 franc

10 francs	Hercules group.	Rev. Value.
5 francs	The Sower.	Same.
1 franc	Same.	Same.
1/2 franc	Same.	Same.
20 centimes	Liberty head.	Same.
10 centimes	Same.	Same.
5 centimes	Wheat stalk (legend in script).	Same.
1 centime	Same.	Same.

France completely revised its coinage in 1960 by issuing a new "heavy franc" equal in value to 100 of the pre-1960 francs. The buying power of each coin remained the same, but foreigners traveling in France were confused by two five-franc coins, each having a different value: the new 5-franc coin worth approximately the same as a U.S. dollar and the old 5-franc piece worth about one cent. For a while, prices of articles for sale were given in both "NF" (new francs) and "F" (old francs), but today all

69

transactions are in terms of the new franc. Nevertheless, the old coins occasionally turn up in circulation and are available for collectors.

The new coins were redesigned or, to be more exact, earlier designs were brought back into use. The obverse of the 10-franc coin, which is rarely seen in circulation, repeats a design first used more than a century and a half ago at the time of the French Revolution. The obverse shows three figures representing liberty, strength and justice. Above the figures is the legend LIBERTE, EGALITE, FRATERNITE, which has appeared on many French coins over the years. The 5-franc coin shows a sower (said to represent France) spreading seeds of knowledge to the world. This design was previously used on coins from 1898 to 1920 and was also used on many stamps of the period. Liberty heads as devices on French coins also were first used at the time of the Revolution. The citizens wore peaked caps as a symbol of their liberty from the king.

For information about the coins of France, write to:

Monnaie de Paris
11, Quai de Conti
Paris VI, France

100 centimes = 1 franc

5 francs	Head of Prince Rainier III.	Rev. Two figures and coat of arms
1 franc	Same.	Rev. Crown and coat of arms.
50 centimes	Same.	Rev. One figure and coat of arms.
20 centimes	Same.	Same.
10 centimes	Same.	Same.

Monaco, the smallest princely state in the world, has a total area of slightly less than three fifths of a square mile and about 3,500 citizens. Monaco is on the Mediterranean coast, enclosed by France on the other three sides. The principality is famous as a tourist attraction, because of the gambling casino at Monte Carlo.

Stamp collectors know Monaco through its colorful stamp issues, but many coin collectors are not aware of the fact that there have been issues of coins as well. French money is the official currency, and the coins in circulation are French. Neverthe-less, the Prince of Monaco has the right to issue coins, which he does from time to time. The Monegasque coins are the same value as the French, and the visitor in Monaco can usually get a few specimens for face value by asking the merchants for them. Nearly all coins of Monaco are in good condition because they cannot circulate very far in this tiny country.

The obverse of the current coins shows the portrait of the reigning prince, Rainier III of the House of Grimaldi. The reverse shows the coat of arms of the Grimaldi family supported by monks with swords on the 5-franc and 50-centime pieces. These monks are in memory of the year 1297 when Rainier I de Grimaldi established the family as rulers of Monaco. The Grimaldis took the Genoan fortress by the ruse of entering the castle disguised as Franciscan monks. The legend DEO JUVANTE which appears an each of the coins means "With God's help."

100 centimes = 1 franc

100 francs	Heads of four Belgian kings.	Rev. Coat of arms.
50 francs	Mercury head.	Rev. Lion with tablets of law.
20 francs	Same.	Same.
5 francs	Ceres head.	Rev. Oak branch.
1 franc	Same.	Same.
50 centimes	Miner's head.	Rev. Value.
25 centimes	Crowned monogram.	Same.

Belgium did not become a nation until 1830, having been passed from Austria to Spain to France as part of the Netherlands over the preceding centuries. Belgium is a constitutional monarchy and Baudouin, the present King, has been on the throne since 1951. Unlike most kings, Baudouin does not have his portrait or name on the regular coin issues, although his likeness has appeared on special issues such as the 1960 50-franc coin struck to commemorate his wedding to Fabiola of Aragon (Spain). The new 25-centime coin first issued in 1964 has his monogram, "B."

The largest Belgian denomination, the hundred-franc piece, is a history lesson in itself because it shows Baudouin's four predecessors—from right to left, Leopold I (1831–65), Leopold II (1865–1909), Albert (1909–34) and Leopold III (1934–50). The reverse shows the Belgian coat of arms, a rampant lion rearing up on hind legs, the forelegs extended one above the other. The two crossed scepters behind the shield symbolize the King's position as the nation's ruler and supreme judge. Below the shield is the Order of Leopold, Belgium's most distinguished decoration. The 100-franc coin is not often seen in circulation, as the face value is equivalent to 2 U.S. dollars.

The lower-value coins show Mercury (god of commerce and trade), Ceres (goddess of grain and agriculture) and a modern miner (for industry) representing the main factors in Belgium's economy.

Belgium has two official languages, French and Flemish, and either the coins show the name of the country in both languages, BELGIQUE-BELGIE, or the same design is issued in approximately equal numbers in each language.

For information about coins of Belgium, write to:

> Banque Nationale de Belgique, Caisse Central
> 5, Boulevard de Berlaimont
> Bruxelles 1, Belgium

100 centimes = 1 franc

100 francs	Head of Grand Duke Jean.	Rev. Coat of arms of the Grand Duke.
1 franc	Same.	Rev. Value.
25 centimes	Coat of arms.	Same.

Luxembourg is another small state that issues its own coins and currency. Unlike Monaco, however, the Luxembourg money is the nation's official currency and is actually in circulation. Luxembourg currency is at par with the Belgian and, in fact, Belgian money is also in use throughout the Grand Duchy. The official language is French, but nearly everyone speaks Letzeburgesch, a local dialect of German origin. On some coins the name of the country is spelled LETZEBURG, on others the French LUXEMBOURG is used.

The 25-centime coin shows the coat of arms, which dates from the thirteenth century, a rampant red lion on a field of blue and white stripes. The man stirring or "puddling" iron on the 1-franc coin is a tribute to the fact that Luxembourg, in spite of its size, is the world's eighth largest steel producer.

The present ruler is Grand Duke Jean, who succeeded his mother, Charlotte, in 1964. Coins of both rulers are now in circulation.

For information about coins of Luxembourg, write to:

Caisse Generale de l'Etat
3, Avenue de la Liberté,
Luxembourg, Luxembourg

100 cents = 1 guilder

2 1/2 guilders	Head of Queen Juliana.	Rev. Lion.
1 guilder	Same.	Same.
25 cents	Same.	Rev. Value.
10 cents	Same.	Same.
5 cents	Same.	Rev. Orange branch and value.
1 cent	Same.	Rev. Value.

During the Middle Ages, the Netherlands came under the rule of the King of Spain. The burghers objected to being ruled from distant Spain, and the seven northern provinces joined together in revolt. The leader of the war of liberation was William the Silent, Prince of Orange and founder of the present dynasty. The orange branch on the reverse of the five-cent coin is a tribute to the royal line. The coat of arms shows a rampant lion holding a sword and a sheaf of seven arrows, representing the seven original provinces which joined in the battle for independence. The two highest value coins have lettered edges, GOD ZIJ MET ONS, "God be with us."

The obverse of all the current Dutch coins shows the portrait of Queen Juliana whose reign began in 1948. All of the denomi-

77

nations from 2½ guilders to the one cent can be found in circulation, although the one cent, equal in value to about an English farthing or one fourth of a U.S. cent, is not used so much any more.

100 ore = 1 krone

5 kroner	Head of Frederick IX.	Rev. Coat of arms in wreath.
1 krone	Same.	Same.
25 ore	Monogram.	Rev. Value in wreath (center-hole planchet).
10 ore	Same.	Same.
5 ore	Same.	Same.
2 ore	Same.	Same.
1 ore	Same.	Same.

The most striking feature of Denmark's coinage is the elaborate shield on the reverse of the 1-krone and 5-kroner pieces. If you study an unworn coin carefully, you can count thirteen distinct and different coats of arms representing areas now part of modern Denmark or lands once ruled or claimed by Danish kings.

In the first quarter, at upper left, are three crowned lions *passant* (walking with the forepaw raised), the arms of Denmark proper since the twelfth century. At upper right are two lions *passant,* the emblem of Schleswig. The third quarter at lower left is itself divided into three parts—three crowns for Sweden (under Danish kings 1397–1521), a ram *passant* for the Faeroes Islands and a seated bear for Greenland. In the fourth quarter is a lion *passant* with ten hearts in the field below representing Gothland and a wivern, a two-legged, winged dragon with a

79

barbed tail. This strange creature is the emblem of Vandalia and exists only as a heraldic device.

If you use a magnifying glass, you will see that an escutcheon, an additional small shield, is superimposed on the main one. This second shield is also quartered and shows three nettle leaves for Holstein, a swan for Stormerk, a mounted rider (chevalier) for Ditmarsh, and a horse's head for Lauenburg.

Almost lost in all this is one more tiny shield divided down the middle with two bars for Oldenburg and a cross for Delmenhorst.

The lower denomination coins show the king's cipher or monogram, FR IX, below a royal crown. An interesting sidelight to Danish coinage is that since 1513 the kings have been alternately named Frederick and Christian. This tradition is likely to be broken in the future, however, as the present king, Frederick IX, has only daughters.

For information about coins of Denmark, write to:

Danmarks Nationalbank
Copenhagen, Denmark

100 ore = 1 krona

5 kronor	Head of King Gustav VI Adolf.	Rev. Coat of arms.
2 kronor	Same.	Same.
1 krona	Same.	Same.
50 ore	Crowned monogram.	Rev. Value.
25 ore	Same.	Same.
10 ore	Same.	Same.
5 ore	Incuse crown and inscription.	Same.
2 ore	Same.	Same.
1 ore	Same.	Same.

Sweden is world renowned for its leadership in the field of modern design, and even Sweden's coins depart from traditional appearances. The 1-, 2- and 5-kroner pieces show an angular, "modernistic" portrait of the King. Compare this portrait with the usual type of portrait on the commemorative 5-kroner piece illustrated. The lowest value coins are unusual in that the design and lettering are sunk below the surface of the planchet rather than being raised up from it as on other modern coinages. This

Commemorative   5-kroner   piece

has the very practical advantage of protecting the design from wearing down in circulation. The 10-, 25- and 50-öre pieces are noteworthy for the simplicity and pleasing arrangement of the King's monogram.

The reverse of the high-value coins shows the three-crowns device, which we have seen already on Denmark's coat of arms, and the Folkunge lion, an even older Swedish device dating to the thirteenth century. The King's motto, PLINKTEN FRAMFOR ALLT, means "Obligation before everything."

For information about coins of Sweden, write to:

Sveriges Riksbank
Stockholm, Sweden

$$100 \text{ ore} = 1 \text{ krone}$$

5 kroner	Head of King Olav V.	Rev. Coat of arms.
1 krone	Same.	Rev. Horse.
50 ore	Same.	Rev. Dog.
25 ore	Same.	Rev. Bird.
10 ore	Monogram.	Rev. Bee.
5 ore	Head.	Rev. Moose.
2 ore	Monogram.	Rev. Chicken.
1 ore	Same.	Rev. Squirrel.

The Norwegian five-kroner piece follows the practice of Denmark and Sweden in showing the king's portrait on one side with the coat of arms on the reverse. Norway's coat of arms is a rampant lion wearing the crown of St. Olaf and holding a battle axe. From 1381 until 1814 Norway was ruled by the Danes, and from 1814 until 1905 was united with Sweden. Even during these periods, coins struck for Norway under the Danish or Swedish kings had the distinctive Norwegian lion on the reverse. The motto ALT FOR NORGE means "Everything for Norway."

The rest of the Norwegian coins feature animals, ranging from a bee to a moose. These animal designs, first issued in 1958, have won the approval of collectors everywhere.

The three Scandinavian countries use the same monetary unit, but in Denmark and Norway it is spelled "krone/kroner" and is equivalent to approximately 15 cents U.S., while in Sweden the spelling is "krona/kronor," and its value is about 20 cents U.S.

For information about coins of Norway, write to:

Norges Bank
Oslo, Norway

100 pennia = 1 markka

1 markka	Coat of arms.	Rev. Value, background of trees.
50 pennia	Coat of arms.	Rev. Value and tree.
20 pennia	Same.	Same.
10 pennia	Same.	Same.
5 pennia	Coat of arms of St. Henry.	Rev. Value.
1 penni	Same.	Same.

The Finns call their country "Suomi," the Land of Marshes (SUOMEN TASAVALTA−Republic of Finland). Outsiders call it Finland from Fennland, fenn being another name for swamp. Finland was part of the kindom of Sweden until 1809, when it became a grand duchy under the Russian czars. It has been an independent republic since 1919. Finland's coins are easily recognized, as it is the only nation in the world using pennia and markka as coin denominations.

Finland's coat of arms is a rampant lion standing on one sword and brandishing another. The trees on the reverses are in tribute to Finland's forests, which are so much a feature of the land and a source of supply for the nation's important lumber industry. The single tree on the fifty-pennia coin is a dwarf birch of the type found just at the northern timber line.

The two lower value coins show the arms of St. Henry. When the pagan Finns were conquered by the Christian Swedes in 1157, King Eric IX left Bishop Henry with them as a missionary. The Finns martyred the bishop, but later made him their patron saint.

For information about coins of Finland, write to:

Suomen Pankki—Finlands Bank
Helsinki, Finland

100 pfennigs = 1 mark

5 marks	Eagle.	Rev. Value.
2 marks	Head of Max Planck.	Rev. Eagle.
1 mark	Eagle.	Rev. Value between oak leaves.
50 pfennigs	Woman planting oak tree.	Rev. Value.
10 pfennigs	Twig with five oak leaves.	Same.
5 pfennigs	Same.	Same.
2 pfennigs	Same.	Same.
1 pfennig	Same.	Same.

Until 1871, Germany was made up of dozens of independent kingdoms, principalities, grand duchies, duchies, margraviates, and free cities which had separate rulers, laws, taxes, armies and coinage. Even after the formation of the German Empire in 1871, distinctive coins were still issued by twenty-five states and cities. Collectors specializing in old German coins are faced with the task of sorting out this profusion of issues. Since 1918, how-

87

ever, one federal coinage has been in use for the whole country. Only the post-World War II coins illustrated here are in circulation today.

The eagle shown on the 5-mark piece is the emblem of the German Federal Republic (West Germany). When seen in color, the eagle is black on a golden background. The word "mark" was originally used to denote a certain weight and came into use as a monetary unit during the last century. The man honored on the 2-mark piece is Max Planck (1858–1947), a German physicist and Nobel Prize winner who developed the quantum theory, a discovery dealing with the absorption and radiation of energy.

For information about coins of Germany, write to:

Staatliche Munze Karlsruhe
Stephanienstrasse 28
Karlsruhe, Germany

100 groschen = 1 schilling

10 schillings	Head of girl.	Rev. Coat of arms.
5 schillings	Lipizaner stallion and rider.	Same.
1 schilling	Edelweiss flowers.	Rev. Value.
50 groschen	Shield.	Same.
10 groschen	Eagle.	Same.
5 groschen	Same.	Same.
2 groschen	Same.	Same.

Austria's modern coins provide an excellent example of how coin engravers are able to indicate different colors although the surface of the coin is a single color—that of the metal. The Austrian coat of arms is a shield with a red band at the top, a white band across the center and another red band at the bottom. More than three hundred years ago, a system was devised wherein lines and dots represent the actual colors of coats of arms on coinage. Fine vertical lines mean red, and no markings at all mean white or silver. Now, can you see the red and white shield in the picture? The other colors that can be shown heraldically are gold or yellow (dots), blue (horizontal lines), black (cross-hatched horizontal and vertical lines), green (diagonal lines descending to the right) and purple (diagonal lines descending to the left).

The girl on the 10-schilling coin is wearing the traditional headdress of *Nieder Oesterreich,* Lower Austria, a province near Vienna. The 1-schilling piece bears a sprig of edelweiss blossoms. The white stallion with his rider decked out in eighteenth-century costume is one of the famed Lipizaner horses of the Spanish Riding School in Vienna. These superbly trained horses have been seen on tour in many countries of the world. Eagles have been used on many Austrian coins over the years. On coins issued since the end of World War II, a broken chain attached to the eagle's legs symbolizes the country's new freedom.

For information about coins of Austria, write to:

Osterreichischen Hauptmunzamter
Am Heumarht 1, Postfach 225
Vienna 14, Austria

100 centimes = 1 franc

5 francs	Bust of William Tell.	Rev. Coat of arms.
2 francs	Helvetia standing.	Rev. Value in wreath.
1 franc	Same.	Same.
1/2 franc	Same.	Same.
20 centimes	Head of Helvetia.	Same.
10 centimes	Same.	Same.
5 centimes	Same.	Same.
2 centimes	Helvetian cross.	Rev. Value and wheat stalk.
1 centime	Same.	Same.

Switzerland is a peaceful little nation whose citizens cling to tradition and age-old crafts and where change comes slowly. The nation's coins are evidence of this attitude, as many of the designs have remained the same for nearly a century. The 1964 2-franc piece illustrated here shows exactly the same figure of Helvetia that was used on the first issue in 1874. On the lower value coins her portrait has been unchanged since 1879. The Swiss emblem, a white cross on a red field, is borne on many of the coins.

The 5-franc coin shows William Tell, Switzerland's national

hero. Tell was the leader of the 1291 alliance of the first three cantons formed to resist the Austrians. But he is much better known for his legendary but unverifiable feat—under the threat of death, he was commanded by the Austrian governor to shoot an apple off his son's head with a bow and arrow.

For information about the coins of Switzerland, write to:

Caisse d'Etat Federale Suisse
Bundesgasse 14
Berne, Switzerland

500 lire	Girl in medieval costume.	Rev. Ships.
100 lire	Head of Italia.	Rev. Woman in classical Grecian costume.
50 lire	Same.	Rev. Vulcan.
20 lire	Same.	Rev. Oak branch.
10 lire	Ancient plow.	Rev. Wheat stalks.
5 lire	Ship's rudder.	Rev. Dolphin.
2 lire	Bee.	Rev. Olive branch.
1 lira	Scales.	Rev. Cornucopia.

Italian coinage began about 350 B.C. in the days of the ancient Romans. The Romans struck very large quantities of coins, mostly bearing portraits of the reigning emperor with gods, goddesses or personifications on the reverse.

In the style of the ancient coins, three of the modern Italian coins show the head of Italia, a personification representing the goodness and abundance of the land. The woman in the Grecian dress on the reverse of the 100-lire coin is the Greek goddess Athena. According to ancient myth, Athena bestowed the olive tree on the early Greeks who in turn introduced it into Italy. The reverse of the 50-lire piece shows Vulcan, the old Roman god of fire and metalworking. The 20-lire reverse displays an oak branch, a traditional emblem for strength. The artist who planned these coins chose his designs to convey the idea that agriculture and manufacturing mean strength for the land of Italy.

The lower value coins also borrow symbols used on coins in ancient times. These are a plow and wheat stalks (agriculture); a ship's rudder and a dolphin (seafaring); a bee (hard work) and an olive branch; scales and a cornucopia, or horn-of-plenty, which are the emblems of Moneta, Roman goddess of money and minting.

The 500-lire coin also has a motif borrowed from earlier times, but in this case from the Renaissance, about A.D. 1500. On the obverse is a girl in the dress of the period. The reverse shows three sailing ships, the fleet in which Christopher Columbus discovered the New World. Although Columbus sailed for Ferdinand and Isabella of Spain, he was an Italian from Genoa. The date of issue of the 500-lire coins is on the edge with the inscription REPUBLICA ITALIANA rather than the usual position on one of the faces of the coin.

For information about coins of Italy, write to:

Banca d'Italia
Via Nazionale 91
Rome, Italy

500 lire	Bust of Pope Paul VI.	Rev. Papal coat of arms.
100 lire	Same.	Rev. Fides (Faith).
50 lire	Same.	Rev. Spes (Hope).
20 lire	Same.	Rev. Caritas (Charity).
10 lire	Same.	Rev. Prudentia (Prudence).
5 lire	Same.	Rev. Iustitia (Justice).
2 lire	Papal arms.	Rev. Fortitudo (Fortitude).
1 lira	Same.	Rev. Temperantia (Temperance).

The Vatican City is a sovereign state, one sixth of a square mile in area, located near the center of Rome. It is the home of the Pope, the spiritual leader of Catholics throughout the world. The papal city has its own stamps and coins, its own newspaper and broadcasting station. The Vatican coins have the same value as the regular Italian coins and, by arrangement with the Italian government, are legal tender throughout Italy. Thus, it is possible occasionally to find Vatican coins in circulation anywhere in Italy, although much more likely in Rome or at the Vatican itself.

Coins of the Vatican City show a portrait of the reigning Pope and on some denominations his personal coat of arms. You can also see the Pope's Tiara, or triple crown, symbolizing his functions as teacher, lawgiver and judge. The crossed keys below the crown stand for the Keys of the Kingdom of Heaven.

The reverses of the lower value coins have personifications of virtues. They are identified on the coins by their Latin names, but you can find the English translations in the listing above.

For information about coins of Vatican City, write to:

Stato della Città del Vaticano
Ufficio di Segreteria
Città del Vaticano

100 centimos = 1 peseta

50 pesetas	Head of Generalissimo Franco.	Rev. Eagle and shield of arms.
25 pesetas	Same.	Same.
5 pesetas	Same.	Same.
2 1/2 pesetas	Same.	Same.
1 peseta	Same.	Rev. Arms and value.
50 centimos	Shields of Castile, León, Aragon, Navarre.	Rev. Anchor and steering wheel.
10 centimos	Head of Generalissimo Franco.	Rev. Value in wreath.

While the Spanish state is officially a kingdom, at present the throne is vacant. The portrait on Spanish coins is that of the chief of state, Generalissimo Francisco Franco, who has held his post since 1936. The kingdom of Spain came into being in 1516 and the devices in the coat of arms stand for the old, separate kingdoms—the castle for Castile, a lion for León, red and yellow vertical stripes for Aragon, chains for Navarre, and squeezed in at the bottom of the shield a pomegranate for the Moorish kingdom of Granada.

The shield on the 2½- and 1-peseta coins is flanked by two

97

columns, the Pillars of Hercules, representing the Rock of Gibraltar and Punta Leone, which mark the western end of the Mediterranean Sea. This was the limit of the ancient world. After the discovery of America and its riches, the pillar device was adopted for the Spanish seal with the motto PLUS ULTRA, "something beyond."

For information about coins of Spain, write to:

Fabrica Nacional de Moneda y Timbre
Jorge Juan 106
Madrid, Spain

100 centavos = 1 escudo

10 escudos	Sailing ship.	Rev. Coat of arms and globe.
5 escudos	Sailing ship.	Rev. Coat of arms.
2 1/2 escudos	Same.	Same.
1 escudo	Head of Republic.	Rev. Coat of arms and value.
50 centavos	Same.	Same.
20 centavos	Cross of Redemption.	Rev. Value.
10 centavos	Same.	Same.

The devices on Portugal's coins serve to extol her past greatness as a seafaring nation. The sailing ships are the type used by Vasco da Gama on his voyage to India by way of the Cape of Good Hope at the southern tip of Africa. The discovery in 1498

99

of this sea route to India enabled the Portuguese to deal directly with the sources of spices, precious stones and other exotic products then in great demand in Europe. During the sixteenth century, little Portugal was Europe's leading trading nation and naval power. On the reverse of the 10-escudo piece is an armillary sphere, an ancient nautical instrument.

The coat of arms shows the Cross of Redemption made up of five shields, each with five roundels (circular ornaments) arranged in a diagonal cross. The Cross is in the center of a shield with a border containing seven small castles.

The value of the escudo has been stable, and the basic coin designs have not changed much over the years. Visitors to Portugal can find twenty- or thirty-year-old coins still in circulation.

100 kopecks = 1 ruble

1 ruble	Hammer and sickle emblem on globe within wreath.	Rev. Value in wreath.
50 kopecks	Same.	Same.
20 kopecks	Same.	Same.
15 kopecks	Same.	Same.
10 kopecks	Same.	Same.
5 kopecks	Same.	Same.
3 kopecks	Same.	Same.
2 kopecks	Same.	Same.
1 kopeck	Same.	Same.

Soviet coins are not too plentiful in the West. Until recently, the government did not allow coins to be sent out of the country, and there are not many tourists going back and forth to carry them out.

The designs on the Soviet coins are the same for all denominations, a hammer and sickle representing industrial and agricultural workers. The wreath is wrapped with a ribbon at the bottom, and there is one band of ribbon for each of the fifteen republics of the Union of Soviet Socialist Republics (U.S.S.R.).

For information about coins of Russia, write to:

Bank for Foreign Trade of the U.S.S.R.
Neglinnaya 12
Moscow, K-16, U.S.S.R.

100 lepta = 1 drachma

10 drachmai	Head of King Constantine.	Rev. Coat of arms.
5 drachmai	Same.	Same.
2 drachmai	Same.	Same.
1 drachma	Same.	Same.
50 lepta	Same.	Same.
20 lepta	Crown and laurel wreath.	Rev. Olive branch.
10 lepta	Same.	Rev. Bunch of grapes.
5 lepta	Same.	Rev. Stalk of wheat.

The present king of Greece, Constantine II, came to the throne upon the death of his father in 1964. He has been living in exile since December, 1967. Many of the coins in circulation are still those with portraits of the late King Paul. The reverse shows the Greek coat of arms—a white cross on a blue shield.

The lower-value coins bear olives, grapes and wheat, the principal agricultural products of the country. The outstanding feature of these coins, however, is the center-hole planchets. The center holes are a device to conserve metal, are decorative and hard to counterfeit, and there is no chance of mistaking a low-value coin for one of the higher denominations.

For information about coins of Greece, write to:

Bank of Greece, Cash Dept.,
P.O. Box 105
Athens, Greece

100 agorot = 1 pound

1 pound	Menorah.	Rev. Value
half pound	Same.	Same.
25 agorot	Kythora (lyra).	Same.
10 agorot	Palm tree with date clusters.	Same.
5 agorot	Pomegranates.	Same.
1 agora	Barley stalks.	Same.

Although Israel is a new nation, having become an independent republic on May 14, 1948, all of its coin designs are replicas of emblems used on the coins of ancient Israel (c. 40 B.C.–A.D. 135). The dates, which are shown in Hebrew characters, are according to the Hebrew calendar, which is figured from the time of Adam. Thus, 1948, the year of independence, is given as 5708, and 1967 as the year 5727.

The menorah, or seven-branched candlestick, brought into use by Moses and long an emblem of the Jewish people, is now the coat of arms of the new state.

In addition to the regular-issue coins which are found in circulation, Israel has issued several commemorative one-pound and five-pound coins. The commemoratives are all issued in limited quantities and sold at a premium over the face value. The premium is not great when the coins are first released, but because of the limited supply and their attractiveness for collectors, some of the older issues now sell for comparatively high prices.

For information about coins of Israel, write to:

Israel Government Coins & Medals Corp., Ltd.
11 Keren Hayesod St.
Jerusalem, Israel
or Israel Government Coins & Medals Corp., Ltd.
850 Third Ave., N.Y., N.Y.

GHANA

10 shillings	Head of Kwame Nkrumah.	Rev. Star.
2 shillings	Same.	Same.
1 shilling	Same.	Same.
6 pence	Same.	Same.
3 pence	Same.	Same.
1 penny	Same.	Same.
halfpenny	Same.	Same.

MALI

25 francs	Lion head.	Rev. Value.
10 francs	Horse head.	Same.
5 francs	Hippopotamus head.	Same.

Since the end of World War II, the independence movement in Africa has given birth to many new nations and ended European domination of the continent. Although the new nations have been quick to issue their own postage stamps and paper currency, new coinages in many cases have had to wait while available funds were used for more urgent projects. Not many collectors have yet acquired coins even from those countries that have replaced their colonial issues with new designs, but as commerce and travel between Africa and the rest of the world increase, certainly more of the new coins will find their way into collections.

Ghana, formerly Britain's Gold Coast colony, was the first of the new African nations, becoming an independent state on March 6, 1957. Prior to independence, the Gold Coast, along with other nearby colonies, used shilling and pence coins struck for British West Africa. The first issue after independence continued the same denominations, but in place of the portrait and titles of the British sovereign, the coins showed the portrait of the head of state, Kwame Nkrumah (since deposed) with the legend CIVITATIS GHANIENSIS CONDITOR, "Founder of the state of Ghana." The name Ghana was taken in the belief that the inhabitants are descended from the great Negro Kingdom of Ghana that flourished in the area from A.D. 800 to 1240. The reverse of the new coinage shows a five-pointed star described as the "lodestar [guiding star] of African independence," an appropriate title for the first of the new nations.

The Republic of Mali is a former French colony not far from Ghana in the western bulge of Africa. As a colony the area was known as French Sudan and with other nearby colonies used franc and centime coins struck for French West Africa. After achieving independence, the new country continued the franc denomination with new design types. The hippopotamus on the 5-franc piece is the only instance of this animal appearing on a coin. The area that is now Mali was also a part of the Kingdom

107

of Ghana in earlier centuries. This ancient kingdom was destroyed by the Moslem empire of Mali in the mid-thirteenth century, and again a new republic took its name from an older empire.

The following new nations have recently issued coins which have not yet become widely available: Burundi, Cameroons, Central African Republic, Congo (Katanga), Gabon, Guinea, Malagasy, Malawi, Nigeria, Rwanda, Sierra Leone, Tanzania, Togo, West African States, Zambia.

100 cents = 1 rand

1 rand	Bust of Jan Van Riebeeck.	Rev. Leaping springbok.
50 cents	Same.	Rev. Native flowers—lily, sterilitzia, agapanthus.
20 cents	Same.	Rev. Protea plant (evergreen shrubs, dense flower head).
10 cents	Same.	Rev. Aloe plant.
5 cents	Same.	Rev. Blue crane.
2 cents	Same.	Rev. Black wildebeest.
1 cent	Same.	Rev. Two sparrows on tree branch.

Although South Africa withdrew from the British Commonwealth and became an independent republic as recently as 1961, the nation has had its own mint and a history of several decades of independent coinage. South Africa also abandoned the pound, shilling and pence system it had used in favor of a new decimal currency based on a rand of 100 cents. The denomination comes from the name Witwatersrand, or "Rand," as it is called locally, the area in South Africa where the world's richest gold fields are located.

The obverse on all denominations shows the bust of Jan Van Riebeeck, who in 1652, along with seventy Dutch burghers, founded the first permanent settlement at the Cape of Good Hope. As South Africa has two official languages, Afrikaans and English, each denomination is issued with the name of the country spelled SUID-AFRIKA on approximately half the coins and SOUTH AFRICA on the balance. The reverses show animals and plants native to the country.

Since South Africa does its own minting, most of the older coins have been melted down and restruck, leaving only the rand and cent coins in circulation.

For information about coins of South Africa, write to:

South African Mint
P.O. Box 464
Pretoria, South Africa

100 yen	Cherry blossoms.	Rev. Value.
50 yen	Same.	Same (center-hole planchet).
10 yen	Temple.	Same.
5 yen	Same.	Same.
1 yen	Same.	Same.

Until nearly the end of the nineteenth century, Japan's coins had quite a different appearance than we are accustomed to. The silver coins were rectangular and the bronze, although mostly round, were cast pieces with a square center hole. Naturally, the inscriptions were in Japanese, just as they are today. In recent years, however, the Japanese have used Western-style numerals to indicate the values of their coins—a great help for any foreigner traveling in Japan.

Most of the coin designs feature flowers and plants; the Japanese are noted for their skill in creating artistic arrangements using these elements. One exception is the 10-yen piece,

111

which has a pictorial representation of the temple at Nara, the chief Buddhist center of early Japan.

In the Japanese currency system 1 yen equals 100 sen, but since the yen itself is equal only to about one third of a U.S. cent (less than a British halfpenny), there is no use for sen coins and they are no longer made.

100 cents = 10 chiao = 1 yuan (dollar)

5 chiao	Bust of Dr. Sun Yat-sen.	Rev. Map of Formosa.
2 chiao	Same.	Same.
1 chiao	Same.	Same.

China is divided between the Communist mainland and the Nationalist government centered on the island of Taiwan (also called Formosa). On their coins, the Nationalist Chinese have continued a design first used on the mainland in 1912, a portrait of Dr. Sun Yat-sen, called "Father of the Revolution" for his role in overthrowing the Manchu emperor to establish the Chinese

1965 issue of commemoratives

113

Republic. The reverse of all denominations shows a map of Taiwan.

In addition to the regular coins in daily use, there was a 1965 issue of commemoratives to mark the hundredth anniversary of the birth of Dr. Sun Yat-sen. These commemoratives did not enter circulation, however, and are only available at a premium from coin dealers.

100 cents = 1 dollar

1 dollar	Crowned bust of Queen Elizabeth II.	Rev. Lion holding globe.
50 cents	Same.	Rev. Chinese characters.
10 cents	Same.	Same.
5 cents	Same.	Same.

Hong Kong is a British Crown Colony, but its population is over 98 percent Chinese. Hong Kong is one of the most strategic seaports in the world, but tourists who visit remember it best for its scenic location on a beautiful natural harbor and as a shopper's paradise with a great variety of wares at bargain prices.

The colony has had its own distinctive coinage since 1866, and the present coins, like all the earlier ones, show the head of the reigning British monarch. The reverses give the value and the name of the colony in both English and Chinese characters. At the top and bottom are HSIANG and CHIANG, the Chinese name for Hong Kong. The characters at the side give the denomination (read from right to left in Chinese)—I YUAN, one dollar; WU HAO, five tenths (parts of a dollar); I HAO, one tenth; and WU HSIEN, five cents.

115

1 dollar = 100 cents

50 cents	Portrait of Queen Elizabeth II.	Rev. Coat of arms supported by a kangaroo and an emu.
20 cents	Same.	Rev. Platypus swimming.
10 cents	Same.	Rev. Male lyre bird.
5 cents	Same.	Rev. Spiny anteater.
2 cents	Same.	Rev. Frilled lizard.
1 cent	Same.	Rev. Feather-tailed glider.

Australia is a fully independent self-governing nation within the British Commonwealth of Nations, and the obverses of all her coins bear the portrait of Queen Elizabeth of Great Britain. The reverse of the 50-cent piece shows Australia's coat of arms, each of the six devices representing one of the original colonies: New South Wales (a cross charged with a lion and four stars); Victoria (a crown and the Southern Cross constellation); Queensland (a Maltese cross and Imperial crown); South Australia (an Australian piping shrike on a perch); Western Australia (black swan); and Tasmania (lion passant). The reverses of the other denominations depict animals native to Australia.

Most plentiful coin in Australia, before the change to the decimal system, was this penny showing the head of young Queen Elizabeth on the obverse and a leaping kangaroo on the reverse.

The duck-billed platypus on the 20-cent piece is a furred creature which lays eggs and represents a stage of evolution from the reptile to the mammal. With webbed feet and hard snout, the platypus dives into water and hunts for food like a duck. The other coins show a lyre bird, a spiny anteater, a frilled lizard and a feather-tailed glider, sometimes called a flying mouse.

In early 1966 Australia replaced the traditional pound, shilling and pence values inherited from the currency of Great Britain with a decimal system of dollars and cents. Such a changeover meant that all the nation's cash registers, adding machines, coin-operated vending machines, etc., had to be mechanically modified to the new denominations. The Australian government itself paid for most of the expenses necessary to the conversion.

Tremendous quantities of the new coins were prepared in advance of the changeover, and the older shillings and pence will be melted down and recoined in the new denominations as quickly as possible. Nevertheless, enough of the old coins will be kept as souvenirs and by numismatists in Australia to ensure their being available for collections for some time to come.

For information about coins of Australia, write to:

Royal Australian Mint
Department of the Treasury
Canberra, A.C.T.
Australia

NEW ZEALAND

1 dollar = 100 cents

1 dollar	Portrait of Queen Elizabeth II.	Rev. Coat of arms.
50 cents	Same.	Rev. Sailing ship *Endeavour*.
20 cents	Same.	Rev. Kiwi bird.
10 cents	Same.	Rev. Maori carved head.
5 cents	Same.	Rev. Tuatara lizard.
2 cents	Same.	Rev. Kowhai flowers.
1 cent	Same.	Rev. Fern leaf.

Although settled by the English, New Zealand owes its name to a Dutchman, Abel Tasman, who discovered the land in 1642 and named it "Nieuw Zeeland" after one of the Dutch provinces.

New Zealand recognizes the British sovereign as its ruler, and the current coins show the head of Queen Elizabeth II.

The dollar reverse shows New Zealand's coat of arms—three galleys with sails furled and oars in motion in the center, four stars in the upper left quarter, a fleece in the upper right, a sheaf of wheat at lower left, and crossed hammers at lower right. Captain James Cook's sailing ship *Endeavour* appears on the 50-cent piece. Cook explored the islands extensively in 1769, claiming them for Britain. Native Maori culture is represented on the 10-cent coin, which features a carved head. The other four coins show some of New Zealand's distinctive animals and flowers. The kiwi, New Zealand's national bird, cannot fly. It has a long curved beak, hairlike feathers, no tail, and only rudimentary wings. Although only the size of an ordinary chicken, the kiwi lays a one-pound egg, eight times larger than a hen's, and the male bird hatches it! The tuatara lizard, an unusual creature, was so named because it has "peaks on its back." Found only on offshore islands, the tuatara is protected by law and is thought to be the last survivor and descendant of prehistoric giant reptiles. The kowhai, described as New Zealand's unofficial flower, blooms on one of the country's few deciduous trees. The fern leaf is one of New Zealand's best-known emblems.

For information about coins of New Zealand, write to:

The Treasury, Private Bag
Lambton Quay
Wellington, New Zealand

SOUTH PACIFIC ISLANDS

FIJI

1 florin	Crowned bust of Queen Elizabeth II.	Rev. Coat of arms.
1 shilling	Same.	Rev. Boat.
6 pence	Same.	Rev. Turtle.
3 pence	Same.	Rev. Native hut.
1 penny	Inscription.	Rev. Value.
halfpenny	Same.	Same.

FRENCH POLYNESIA

100 centimes = 1 franc

5 francs	Seated female figure.	Rev. Tropical scene.
2 francs	Same.	Same.
1 franc	Same.	Same.
50 centimes	Same.	Same.

Our tour of the world via its coins ends in the far-off South Sea Islands. Not many years ago, visitors to these islands were a rarity, but the age of jet aircraft has brought these specks of land in the vast Pacific within hours of the rest of the globe and ever-increasing numbers of travelers visit them each year. Even the issues of these islands are coins you *can* collect—with perhaps a little extra effort or a strong urge to travel.

Fiji, a British Crown Colony, is a group of over five hundred islands about a thousand miles north of New Zealand. The coins all carry the portrait or name of the British sovereign. The pieces illustrated show Queen Elizabeth, but coins of her father and even her grandfather are still in use. The reverse of the florin (2 shillings) displays the Fiji coat of arms—an English lion above holding a coconut, and below three sugar canes, a coconut palm, a dove with an olive branch, and a hand (bunch) of bananas. Some of the other coins show native scenes—a hut, a turtle and a catamaran made of logs lashed together and moved by sails.

French Polynesia, an overseas territory of France, is made up of about 130 islands including Tahiti that dot a vast area of the South Pacific to the east of Fiji. The islands are of coral or volcanic origin; many are mountainous, and they are noted for their exceptional beauty.

The reverse design of the coins, which is the same for all denominations, presents a tropical scene with palm trees, boats, mountains, plants and fruits. The figure on the obverse represents Republic, a common device on the coins of France itself, holding a torch and a horn-of-plenty overflowing with fruit.

GLOSSARY

AT PAR—An exchange at equal value of the money of one country in relation to the money of another.

BAND—On a coin, an outlined strip on which words are written.

BASE METAL—Any nonprecious metal such as copper, nickel or aluminum.

CAST COIN—A coin made by pouring molten metal into a mold.

COAT OF ARMS—A shield with a distinctive design on it, chosen as the emblem of a person or a country.

COMMEMORATIVE COIN—A coin that honors a particular event or individual in its design or legend.

CONDITION—The actual physical state of preservation of a coin.

COUNTERFEIT—A fraudulent coin made by unauthorized persons.

DECIMAL SYSTEM—A scheme of coinage in which the coins are based on multiples of 10.

DENOMINATION—The name of a unit of coinage.

DEVICE—An emblematic design on a coin.

DIE—The metal piece used in the coining process to stamp the design onto the planchet.

EDGE—The surface of the thickness of a coin.

FACE VALUE—The legal worth of a coin in the country of issue.

122

FACING—Describing an animal that is shown in profile with its head turned toward the viewer.

HERALDIC—Having to do with coats of arms, which often are the only means of identifying early coins.

INSCRIPTION—The words, letters and legends on a coin.

ISSUE—A set of coins released at the same time.

LABEL—On a coin, an outlined area on which words are written.

MINT MARK—Symbols or letters on a coin indicating the place at which the coin was struck.

MONETARY UNIT—The basic denomination of a coinage system.

NUMISMATICS—The study of coins, from the Greek word *nomisma,* which means "coin."

NUMISMATIST—A collector who is also interested in learning about the history of his coins.

OBVERSE—The "head" side of a coin carrying the portrait or other most important feature of the design.

PASSANT—A heraldic term meaning an animal walking with its right forepaw in the air.

PERSONIFICATION—A human figure meant to show some quality, thing or thought, such as the female head often used on coins to represent "Liberty."

PLANCHET—The blank disc on which the die impresses the coin design.

QUARTER—A division of the shield of a coat of arms. Each division is called a quarter even when the shield is divided into more than four parts.

RAMPANT—A heraldic term meaning an animal rearing up on its hind legs.

REVERSE—The "tail" side of a coin, often showing the denomination.

ROUNDELS—A heraldic term describing circular ornaments as part of a coin design.

STRUCK COIN—A coin made by being stamped under pressure between a pair of dies.

VALUE—What a coin is worth. The "market" value is the price dealers charge for coins offered for sale. The "premium" value is the price over and above face value at which a collector can sell a coin and/or a dealer would buy it.

INDEX

Adam, 104
Africa, 99, 106–08
Albert, King of Belgium, 74
American, 24, 28, 45, 50, 51
American Numismatic Society, 19
Andes Mountains, 56, 57
Animals, 23–24, 27, 28, 29, 31, 34,
  36, 51–52, 53, 55, 59, 63, 65, 66–
  67, 74, 77, 79, 83, 84, 85, 89, 90,
  97, 106, 107, 109, 110, 115, 116,
  117, 120, 121
Apostle of the Indies, 45
Argentina, 51–52, 53, 57
Artigas, José Gervasio, 53
Aruba, 35
Athena (Greek goddess), 94
Atlantic Ocean, 33, 34, 47
Australia, 116–17
Austria, 73, 89–90, 92
Aztec, 29–30

Bahamas, 31–32
Balboa, Vasco Núñez de, 42–43
Baudouin, King, 73–74
Belgium, 73–74
Belize, British Honduras, 49
Bermuda, 33
Bermudez, Juan de, 33
Birds, 23–24, 29, 31, 45, 56, 57, 65,
  87, 88, 89, 90, 97, 101, 116–17,
  118–19
Boats, 27–28, 31, 33, 47, 52, 54, 56,
  63, 93, 94, 97, 99, 109, 120, 121
Bolívar, Simón, 54, 55, 60
Bolivia, 60
Book of the Gospels, 38

Brazil, 50, 53
British Honduras, 49
British West Africa, 107
Brittany, 67
Buenos Aires, 53
Burundi, 108

Cabot, John, 27
Cameroons, 108
Canada, 16, 27–28, 68
Cape of Good Hope, 99, 110
Captaincy General of Guatemala, 40
Caracas, Venezuela, 55
Caribbean, 48
Cartier, Jacques, 27
Catholics, 96
Celtic, 62
Central African Republic, 108
Central America, 40, 45, 46, 47, 49
Ceres (Roman goddess), 74
Channel Islands, 66–68
Charlottesville, Virginia, 25
Chile, 57
China (Chinese), 113–14, 115
Churchill, Sir Winston, 63
Coins: sources for, 13–14; basic facts
  of, 15; handling of, 17; value of,
  18; publications, 19
Coins Magazine, 19
Coin World, 19
Colombia, 42, 54, 55
Columbus, Christopher, 32, 34, 46,
  47, 48, 50, 94
Congo (Katanga), 108
Conquistadores, 30, 43, 45
Constantine II, King, 102

Continental Congress, 25
Córdoba, Francisco Hernández de, 40
Costa Rico, 40, 47
Cross of Redemption, 100
Cuauhtemoc (Aztec emperor), 29–30
Curaçao, 35–36

De Alvarado, Pedro, 45
Declaration of Independence, 25
Da Gama, Vasco, 99–100
De Las Casas, Fray Bartolomé, 45
Denmark, 79–80, 83–84
De Sucre, José Antonio, 56
Díaz, Porfirio, 30
Dominguez, Josefa Ortiz de, 29–30
Dominican Republic, 38–39
Drake, Sir Francis, 63
Dutch. See Netherlands
Duvalier, President of Haiti, 37

East Indies, 34
Ecuador, 54, 57
El Salvador, 40, 46
Elizabeth II, Queen, 27–28, 31–32,
    33, 34, 62, 115, 116, 118, 119, 120,
    121
England. See Great Britain
Eric IX, King, 86
Europe, 25, 43, 100, 107

Fabiola of Aragon, 74
Faeroes Islands, 79
Ferdinand, King, 94
Fiji, 120–21
Finland, 85–86
Fish, 31, 32, 65, 93, 94
Flowers, 32, 34, 45, 63, 89, 109, 110,
    111, 118
Formosa, 113
France (French), 11, 25, 27, 28, 30,
    37, 67, 69–70, 71–72, 73, 74, 107,
    121
Franco, Generalissimo Francisco, 97
Franklin, Benjamin, 26
Frederick IX, King, 80
French Polynesia, 120–21
French Revolution, 70
French Sudan, 107

French West Africa, 107
Fruit, 32, 34, 36, 54, 102, 104, 121

Gabon, 108
Genoa, Italy, 72, 94
George VI, King, 62
German Empire, 87
Ghana, 106–07, 108
Granada, 40, 54, 97
Great Britain, 16, 27–28, 32, 33, 34,
    44, 49, 64–65, 67, 78, 96, 107, 109,
    110, 112, 115, 116, 117, 118, 119,
    121
Greece (Greeks), 94, 102–03
Greenland, 79
Grimaldi, Rainier I de, 72
Guatemala, 40, 44–45, 49
Guernsey, island of, 66–67
Guinea, 108

Haiti, 37, 39
Hamilton, Bermuda, 33
Hebrew, 104
Henry, Bishop of Finland, 86
Henry VIII, King, 64
Hercules, Pillars of, 59, 98
Hispaniola, 37, 38
Honduras, 40, 48
Hong Kong, 115

India, 99–100
Indians, 27, 38, 43, 44–45, 47, 48
Inca, 51, 59
Ireland, 28, 63, 64–65
Isabella, Queen, 94
Irsael, 104–05
Italy (Italians), 11, 63, 93–94

Jamaica, 34
Japan, 111–12
Jefferson, Thomas, 23, 25
Jersey, island of, 66–67
Joachimsthal, Bohemia, 25
Johnson, Lyndon B., 23
Josefa, Doña, 29–30
Juárez, Benito, 29–30
Juliana, Queen, 35, 77
Julian calendar, 44

Kennedy, John F., 23
Keys of the Kingdom of Heaven, 96

Lake Texcoco, 29
Latin, 11, 24–25, 63, 96
Latin America, 38, 55
Lempira (Indian chief), 48
Lend-lease loans, 62
León, Nicaragua, 40
Leopold I of Belgium, 74
Leopold II of Belgium, 74
Leopold III of Belgium, 74
Liberty, 26, 37, 38, 58
Lima, Peru, 59
Lincoln, Abraham, 23–25
Louisiana Territory, 25

Madero, Francisco I., 29–30
Malagasy, 108
Malawi, 108
Mali, 107–08
Maximilian, Archduke, 30
Maya-Quiche civilization, 44
Menorah, 104
Mercury (Roman god), 74
Mexico, 29–30
Middle Ages, 35, 65, 77
Mint marks, 45, 57
Monaco, 71–72
Moneta (Roman goddess), 94
Monte Carlo, 71
Monticello, 23, 25
Morazán, Francisco, 46
Morelos y Pavón, José María, 29–30
Morgan, Henry, 34
Moses, 104
Moslem, 108
Mottoes, 24, 28, 32, 33, 37, 38, 40,
    43, 51, 58, 70, 72, 77, 82, 84, 98
Mt. Chimborazo, 56

Nara, Japan, 112
Netherlands, 73, 77–78, 110, 118
Netherlands Antilles, 35–36
New Guatemala, 45
New World, 25, 45, 48, 94
New Zealand, 118–19, 121

Nicaragua, 40–41
Nigeria, 108
Nkrumah, Kwame, 107
Normandy, 67
North America, 40
Norway, 83–84
Nova Scotia, 28
Numismatic Gazette, The, 19
Numismatic News, 19
Numismatic Scrapbook Magazine, 19
Numismatist, The, 19

Order of Leopold, 74
Orange-Nassau, House of, 35

Pacific Ocean, 43, 47, 121
Panama, 42–43, 54
Panama Canal, 42, 54
Paraguay, 58
Pedrarias, Governor, 43
Peru, 54, 60
Philip II, King of Spain, 59
Planck, Max, 88
Plants, 29, 30, 43, 50, 55, 60, 74, 90,
    94, 102, 104, 111, 121
Pope, the, 96
Port Royal, Jamaica, 34
Portugal, 50, 99–100
Potosí, 59, 60

Quiriga, 44
Quito, Ecuador, 56

Rainier III, Prince, 72
Renaissance, 94
Reptiles, 29, 34, 116, 117
Rock of Gibraltor, 98
Roman Empire, 62, 94
Rome, Italy, 94
Roosevelt, Franklin D., 23–24
Russia. See U.S.S.R.
Rwanda, 108

St. Eustatius, island of, 35
Santiago, Chile, 57
Scotland, 28, 63
Seaby's Coin & Medal Bulletin, 19

Sierra Leone, 108
Somers, Admiral Sir George, 33
South Africa, 109–10
South America, 40, 50, 51, 54, 55, 56, 59, 60
South Pacific Islands, 120–21
Southern Cross Constellation, 50, 116
Spain (Spanish), 11, 30, 32, 33, 37, 38, 40, 43, 45, 46, 47, 48, 49, 50, 51, 53, 54, 55, 56, 57, 59, 60, 73–74, 77, 90, 97–98
Spanish Riding School, Vienna, 90
Sun Yat-Sen, Dr., 113, 114
Sweden, 79, 81–82, 83–84, 85, 86
Switzerland, 91–92

Taiwan, 113, 114
Tanzania, 108
Tasman, Abel, 118
Tell, William, 91–92
Tenochtitlán, Mexico, 29
Togo, 108
Torch of Freedom, 23–24
Tours, France, 67
Trees, 27, 37, 59, 60, 85, 104

U.S.S.R., 85, 101

United States, 16, 23–25, 38, 40, 42, 43, 67, 68, 69, 78, 112
Urraca (Indian chief), 43
Uruguay, 53

Van Riebeeck, Jan, 110
Vatican City, 95–96
Venezuela, 54, 55
Victoria, Queen, 62
Vienna, Austria, 90
Vikings, 64
Voyageurs, 27
Vulcan (Roman god), 94

Washington, D.C., 24
Washington, George, 23
West African States, 108
West Germany, 87–88
West Indies, 34
White House, 25
Whitman Numismatic Journal, 19
William, Prince of Orange, 77
World Coins, 19
World War II, 88, 90, 107

Zambia, 108
Zapotec Indians, 30